THE SECRET LIFE OF
DOCTORS

DR STEPHEN M. KALADEEN

ISBN: 1463744870

ISBN 13 9781463744878

Library Congress Control Number: 2013902033

CreateSpace Independent Publishing Platform

North Charleston, South Carolina

INTRODUCTION

"Doctor, thank you so much for helping my father. How can I ever repay you for saving his life?" The young woman bit her lower lip and tossed her soft, chestnut-colored hair back. She was wearing mulberry-colored lipstick called Yummy Plummy. Leaning closer to me, she crossed her shapely, tanned legs. Then she reached out and gently touched my hand, looking at me expectantly.

I sat back in my office chair, pondering the unspoken message. Finally, I asked her the one thing I needed to know.

"Um...does your dad actually have health insurance?"

DISCLAIMER

This book is entirely a work of fiction. Although it has the feel of some sort of reality, it is just an amalgam of many days working at a hospital mixed with the vivid imaginings of a guy who daydreams in Technicolor.

The truth is that this book isn't even that sexy.

Sometimes; however, you can be *more* sexy by not *trying* to be sexy.

I figure if I use the word 'sex' enough; you are bound to buy the book....

Okay, just buy the book already.

TABLE OF CONTENTS

THE BEGINNING

Ah, there is absolutely nothing better than fooling someone into thinking that you are something that you are not. When I tell people I'm a doctor, they immediately think that I'm some sort of saint. It's especially good at parties. I don't have to exaggerate the importance of my work. I can merely sit back and mention something about some poor cancer patient whom I have treated. I can hold my own with celebrity chefs, artists, millionaires, and all the other buffoons who strive for social standing.

When I began my career, it was almost idyllic. It was very close to that Norman Rockwell vision of the family doc helping out a youngster with an injured teddy bear. Sadly, a new vision has supplanted this old vision of medicine. Teamwork, integrated health systems, and high technology now dominate everything we doctors do.

It's nice that people still think of a doctor as someone akin to a saint. Let's face it, though, anyone who has ever dealt with a coworker or teammate knows that there is a darker side to each of us. My own malignant side manifested itself in a relatively small hospital in Southern Ontario, where I began to work as a family doctor and part-time anesthetist.

The work wasn't terribly hard and it left me with spare time to sit and think. *Idle time and an idle mind really are the devil's playthings.*

—〰—

"You'll feel a tiny pin prick and
then you might die."

THE ANESTHESIA DEPARTMENT

Most of us find that whatever training we received at school rarely prepares us for the real-life challenges that come up at work. Doctors do not accept this fact very well. We spend so much time in school, and we get tested so often that we get this idea: "Hell, I ought to know everything I need to know, as I just spent about eight to twelve years training for the job." I was in this very comfortable position up until a few years ago. What brought my ignorant bliss to an end was my appointment to the Department of Anesthesia at Community Memorial Hospital. This was a small hospital in a small town in Southern Ontario. A group of executives ruled over our hospital and three others. This fact had a tendency to worry us. We were only important to the patients—not anyone with real power. If we needed or wanted something, we often were told that some other hospital was in greater need. It didn't matter if this other hospital was larger or smaller than ours. "So bugger off," they would more or less say. There was also the ugly reality that the administrators might close our hospital to preserve the other hospitals. This was much like a coyote chewing off its trapped leg to preserve the rest of its body.

07:00 Monday morning.

There is an oft-quoted line in super hero movies 'with great power comes great responsibility'. The thing is that the super hero never seems to be all that happy. In a hospital there is always plenty of responsibility to go around. As a younger doctor I had always felt that volunteering for extra work was dangerous. Hanging on the sidelines, grumbling about the emergency schedule, and complaining about the uncomfortable OR chairs—this really did seem to be my forte. The older members of the Department of Anaesthesia understood my disposition toward laziness and accommodated me. The thing is that nothing ever stays the same. Change is inevitable and my own metamorphosis was to be forced upon me at a hospital department meeting. The meeting was in the basement of the hospital. The only thing that distinguished this room from one of the storage rooms was that there was a table there and a small cart with a muffin plate and carafe of coffee.

"Unfortunately, Steve, we had to have an emergency department meeting while you were away in Mexico."

"Oh really? What's this all about? Have they switched us to that cheaper coffee supplier?"

"No."

"Have they switched us to a cheaper drug supplier?"

"No"

"Have they switched us to those cheaper polyester scrub suits?"

"No. Steve, um, Barry here needs a break from being chief of the department. We have been reviewing the records, and it appears that everyone has been the department head except for you."

Truthfully, I had hoped that no one would notice this. My colleague went on: "We therefore had to vote you in. I am truly sorry that you didn't get a chance to vote, as you were in Mexico."

The undemocratic nerve of these guys—holding a vote while I wasn't even in the country! I was about to demand a new vote when Barry mentioned that the vote had been unanimous and my vote would not have made any difference in the outcome. I was therefore stuck with this new position.

"Um, does the hospital pay anything for being department head?"

"No, but there is some prestige associated with being a department head."

"Do I get a special parking space or something like that?"

"No. Actually, Steve, you will have to attend a couple of meetings a week. The hospital doesn't actually pay for your attendance at these meetings, but it is really important that you attend in order to keep things running smoothly."

"What do I get out of this whole deal then?"

"The admiration and respect of your colleagues."

At this point, the three other anesthetists nodded vigorously while chewing their low-fat bran muffins. The muffins were rather dry and chewy. One of the other docs swallowed loudly and at last spoke up.

"Yeah, Steve, you also get the first choice of the muffin plate. When I was chief, I always took the muffin with the chocolate chips in it." I looked at the plate with the muffins on it. There was one left—the one with the chocolate chips in it. Somewhat reluctantly, I took the muffin while the others looked on. As I put it on my paper plate, they smiled. Then Barry, who had previously been the chief, said to me, "Steve, there are a few things we should go over with you before you start the job later this week."

"Oh, what's that?" The muffin was rather good. It had large crystals of sugar on top of it. I wasn't really sure that it was low-fat, but the stress of the meeting had bumped up my metabolic rate. I was thus burning more calories anyway. Barry spoke up.

"Steve, at these meetings you are going to meet all sorts of difficult people—not just pompous surgeons and crabby menopausal nurses."

"You mean there are even worse people at these meetings?"

"Yes, Steve. The worst, by far, is the hospital CEO."

My other colleagues reacted when the CEO was mentioned. Fred, our most senior member, spit his coffee up.

"Yes, Steve. We loathe him."

The others nodded vigorously.

"Yes, Steve. We *fear* and loathe him." Donald, the most reticent of my three colleagues, at last spoke up.

"Steve, this guy hired a consultant who somehow recommended to the hospital board that the CEO salary should be increased from $250,000 to over $400,000. He claimed that this is what he would be paid in the private sector."

I was outraged. "What! If the prick could get paid more in the private sector, then why didn't he leave his current job and get a better- paying job?"

"Why bother changing jobs when all you have to do is get a consultant to recommend a pay raise."

My colleagues then spent the morning briefing me on the hospital situation. The hospital CEO had arrived about two years ago. He had obtained his exalted position through shameless self-promotion, an MBA, and never ever wasting time actually looking after sick people. This fellow had realized that he could make a good living in the Canadian health-care industry, even though he knew nothing about actual health care. He more than made up for his ignorance of health knowledge by frequently displaying a stunning repertoire of health-industry buzz-words and execu-speak.

Barry summed up the others' feelings about the hospital CEO by saying, "Steve, the CEO has single-hand-edly diverted millions of dollars of the hospital's money into consultants, software systems, utilization programs, subcontractors, and executive-pay packages. He is completely immune to medical logic and the normal arguments we use to promote wellness in this community."

"At meetings, he uses 'Jedi mind tricks', which somehow get the doctors to fight among themselves. We don't even have a chance to speak when he's around."

"Not only that, Steve. He is cultivating a whole cadre of laptop-carrying department managers who are running the place now. Doctors don't run hospitals anymore. We are all just tiny cogs in a vast machine that's run by a guy with an MBA who talks nice."

I sipped my weak coffee and picked the sugar crystals off of my muffin. This was serious and I was clearly unprepared for the responsibility.

"Guys, I can't really handle all of this stuff. I'm just a regular doctor like you. The only change I've ever wanted to make at the hospital involved getting more comfortable operating room chairs."

"Steve, we know you have been complaining about the old OR chairs. I think you should pursue this. Actually, your role for our department and the rest of the medical staff is simply to do what you do best."

"What do you mean?"

"Well, Steve, we need someone to buy us some time. There's a young new ER doc who's going to get an MBA. He will graduate in two years. Your job will be to keep things on an even keel until we can somehow get this doctor to be our Chief of Staff. He could then become the hospital CEO. By then, we are hoping that the current CEO will have been promoted to the position of Deputy Minister of Health and have to leave the area."

"So, I'm kind of like that guy dressed up in a bird suit who comes out at half-time during a football game to cheer the crowd on."

"Exactly!"

The other guys nodded in agreement. The muffin had lost its flavor. Suddenly, I needed to go to the bathroom.

—ɯ—

"Don't worry. This will hurt your insurance company more than it will hurt you."

EMERGENCY! WHAT EMERGENCY?

February 3rd, 2012

Memo

To: Front Line Staff.

From: Senior Management Leadership Team.

This memo is to advise staff that, as part of the Community Memorial Hospital Continuous Quality Improvement (CQI) program, we have installed new electronic sensors for our bio-waste disposal system.

The new bio-waste management units do not have a manual control function and are fully automated. They function using new infrared technology. We feel that this new enhanced technology will improve the efficiency of patient management flow by at least 20%.

Sincerely,

Donald Prumt CEO, Community Memorial Hospital

2 weeks later.......

"What we really need is an Emergency Preparedness Plan," said Linda, the hospital manager. She was sitting in the air-conditioned head office of Community Memorial Hospital. The other people in the meeting room nodded in agreement, and a more senior manager added, "What we really need is Emergency Preparedness *Excellence* with an associated Step by Step Incident Management Plan." The Infection Control manager spoke up: "I think that our emergency management preparedness plan must include appropriate Infection Control and a review of our Personal Protective Equipment Applications."

The hospital CEO, who was chairing the meeting, summed up what everyone had said by concluding, "What we really need is to forge a Universal Procedural Standard and a Common Management Template." Everyone nodded in vigorous agreement. The emergency meeting had come about due to a disaster that had occurred in the Community Memorial operating room the day before.

Typically, the disaster had occurred as a result of the confluence of factors involving technology, human frailty, and medical treatment gone awry. The story, embellished to the point that it was almost apocryphal, involved a certain eighty-four-year- old lady who had come to the hospital to have a colonoscopy (bowel examination). Having been prepared for her procedure, she advised the nurse that she was having some bowel cramping and she felt that she had to use the toilet. She was lead to the OR bathroom, where she was at last very much relieved. The problem began when the toilet, which was equipped with an electronic sensor, detected that someone was on the toilet and automatically flushed. The problem was that the woman had used a rather large ball of toilet paper, which kept floating. The automatic sensor sensed the toilet paper ball, and it kept flushing and flushing, causing the toilet to eventually overflow. The OR was thus contaminated with a foul-smelling river that began in a toilet that just wouldn't quit.

The resulting effluent spilled first into the hallway. Then it gradually spread into the scrub room. Some of it actually ventured into an operating room, where doctors were performing minor orthopedic surgery.

Linda, the junior manager who had spoken first at the meeting, described all of this. "You can imagine how difficult and dangerous it was. That's why I declared a state of emergency and activated the emergency response team as per our High Productivity Protocol." The CEO looked a bit puzzled. "What kind of emergency code do you call in this particular case? Is it a code blue or a code red?" "Actually, sir, it's called a code brown." "Oh," he replied curtly.

The manager went on to describe how the emergency had been handled. "To begin with, I set up a command post in my office and quickly met with the head of infection control. Together, we went through a gap analysis, and we realized that one of the main concerns was that there was a possibility that the problem might spread to other areas of the hospital. We thus quarantined off the OR and did not allow anyone to leave before we had developed an appropriate decontamination approach."

"How did the staff handle this? Were you able to develop a human factor analysis?" asked the head of Human Resources. Linda took a deep breath; she had anticipated this rather difficult question.

"Well, at first the staff were cooperative; however, when we didn't let them out because of decontamination issues, they got a bit angry. We had to realign their goals towards a Respectful Crisis Management Outcome. We were able to somewhat improve their cooperation by distributing extra water and juice boxes to the staff and the affected patients. We also distributed extra fans." The HR manager noted that this was very thoughtful. "We also got the Information Technology people involved. First, we attempted to cut off the supply of electricity to the bathroom that had started the problem. This was unsuccessful, as we learned later that the toilet sensors are battery powered." The CEO asked if we had tried anything else to incentivize the staff. "Actually, we tried a variety of other maneuvers, including cutting off the entire water supply to the OR. This worked but when the other toilets wouldn't flush, the staff became even angrier—particularly after we had distributed juice boxes and bottled water before turning off the plumbing."

"After trying the aforementioned procedures, we realized that it had gotten late, so we ordered some takeout food and brainstormed a plan. We needed everyone at the same place so that we could employ some cross platform synergy." Linda went on to describe how the managers, having consumed their takeout dinner, decided to contact the Deputy Medical Officer of Health, who then contacted the Chief of the Centre for Emergency Preparedness and Response at Health Canada. Both of these officials suggested that we contact the Center for Disease Control in Atlanta. We also contacted the World Health Organization in Switzerland. Warming up to her story, Linda became almost breathless. "We brought everyone in on a conference call at the command center at my office. We decided that we should set up a joint municipal, regional, provincial, and federal task force. We also got international assistance from the Red Cross which helped with our network virtualization."

The CEO smiled inwardly, relishing the fact that this crisis would help solidify his large annual bonus and eventual promotion to lead a government task force into 'Hospital Related toilet Disasters – (Toilets –Are They Weapons of Mass Destruction?)'. "Excellent work, Linda. So, how was the problem finally resolved?" "Actually," said Linda. "The staff members who we quarantined were incentivized enough to resolve the problem." After attempting to shut down the malfunctioning bio-waste unit (i.e., the toilet), the staff had someone put on some old rubber boots and go into the contaminated area. "Exactly what did the staff member do to resolve the crisis? Was he in contact with the Centre for Disease Control?" "Actually," said Linda. "He took a plunger and cleared the obstruction in the toilet. Really this was an excellent example of cross platform skills transfer." Linda went on to say that once the toilet had been cleared, the area was sprayed down with disinfectant, and the staff members were directed to change their clothing. Eventually, they all went home.

"By the way, did we follow the Provincial Guidelines Framework for Emergency Management?" The CEO's question summed up the meeting. "Absolutely, sir." Linda was very pleased that she had followed the Provincial Guidelines. The CEO thanked everyone and advised the managerial staff that a Communications Roadmap was critical in this crisis and that this was a true example of synergy and convergence of the intellectual capital of the staff members.

They left the office (temporary command post). Shortly thereafter, a somewhat portly janitor came in to clean out the detritus from the meeting. "Damn electric toilets. I knew they would cause problems," he muttered to him-self. He was carrying a mop and a large toilet plunger that looked like it had been recently used.

—∞—

HELPFUL TIP FROM DR K.........

**Don't ever punch some old guy in the pacemaker
(usually located in the upper Left chest area). It
hurts and you will have a lot to explain to the
Emergency Room doctor.**

THE COMMITTEE BIG LEAGUES

Committee: A group of people that forms when the stupidity of one person won't suffice. (From The Urban Dictionary)

Committee Mentality: The collective stupidity that results when a committee forms. (From The Urban Dictionary)

Committee Whore: Someone who diligently attends committee meetings but whose motives are suspect. They always seem to be up to something underhanded...

Recently, I had an opportunity to go to my hospital Medical Advisory Committee. This is the big committee where all of the heavy-weight doctors and the CEO resolve the difficult problems that come up while running a hospital. This meeting distinguished itself by serving a full dinner, rather than the usual doughnuts and muffins. When I arrived at the evening meeting, I was impressed with the hot and cold buffet. There were salads and chocolate éclairs for desert. I did a swift calculation. If everyone had one éclair, there would be at least three or four left over. Hmm. I suspected that we were being bribed or at least lulled into a sleepy postprandial torpor so that the administration could spring something nasty on us. Resolving to be ever vigilant, I had a salad and two cups of coffee. Consuming carbohydrates was a sign of weakness. I eyed the clock, hoping to secretly grab an éclair at the end of the meeting (when no one was looking).

The meeting was about something called utilization management and a project that the hospital wanted to push forward in this area. I was soon to realize that "utilization management" was an administrative phrase for squeezing as much work as possible out of the doctors and nurses. Apparently, the costs at our hospital were spiraling upward, and the hospital was over a million dollars in debt. This debt had to be rectified somehow.

I had noted that the nurses seemed to be getting a great deal of overtime hours, and I asked if this project would reduce this overtime, as I suspected it was quite costly. A senior manager nodded sagely, "Not exactly, Dr. K. We were staffing for 85 percent bed occupancy, and we are now staffing for 95 percent. So, we probably won't see much savings that way, but it will help somewhat." The manager went on to explain. "This is just one spoke in the wheel of our operating plan, which will reduce our costs and make the hospital look better to the Ministry of Health. It has to do with the hospital's funding formula and our weighted case costs."

I became completely lost in the managerial jargon. I tried to come up with something equally literate to say, but my blood sugar was too low and all I could do was nod my head like one of those dolls that bob up and down on the dashboard of your car. The meeting droned on with much talk of cooperation among staff members and the need for more homecare. Blah, blah, blah. I began to be lulled into a state of rapture as I watched a rather portly specialist stuff down an éclair with sensual abandon. I became convinced that at least one of the older docs had turned off his hearing aid and was preparing to drift off to sleep. *Ah, chocolate.* When the meeting was over, I planned to grab not one but two éclairs—one for the road!

One of the other doctors who had actually been paying attention pointed out that this project had an expected cost of over one hundred thousand dollars. Wait a second. I thought we were trying to save money! In a moment of clarity I realized that the whole chocolate éclair thing had been designed to lull us into indifference. As if on cue, the chief of staff mentioned that if there were no more questions, we should put the project to a vote. I looked around nervously, watching the other members raise their hands in support of the project. This was truly an 'Animal Farm' moment. I quickly raised my hand also, following the herd instinct. Embarrassed, I thought for a moment that we were actually going to start braying, "Four legs good; two legs bad." The chief of staff finally adjourned the meeting. Phew. At least it was over.

Just as I was preparing to make a dash to the pastry table, the CEO approached me and said, "Steve, you seem to be quite interested in Utilization Management. Perhaps I could send you some material. It really is the future of hospital management," Not wanting to seem rude, I gave him my fax number and asked, "Just how much material are you sending?" "It's probably about fifty pages," he replied. "Perhaps you can get your secretary to photocopy the material and just send it to my office." Rather than wearing out the fax machine, I reasoned that I could quickly read over the headings and the pictures, and then give the stuff to my kids to recycle.

Eyeing my watch but not wanting to look too obvious, I edged away from the CEO and meandered to the buffet table. Wait a second! There were no éclairs left. Somehow, in the brief few moments that I had spent with the CEO, some other people had lunged for the desert table. Like a group of vultures, they had picked the table clean! An older staff doctor saw my distressed look. He winked at me while patting his stomach. Fuming, I contemplated giving him the finger, but I decided against it. Instead; I resolved to send him a crabby patient of mine who never gets better and always forgets her pills.

That evening, I began to realize that this committee had some real talent. It was going to be a challenge to even get a reasonable meal. I mulled over my future strategy while I was waiting in the McDonald's drive-through on the way home.

It's going to be a long year....

—∞—

"The problem is that you're overmedicated.
Luckily there are drugs that can help with that."

ORGANIC MEDICINE?

Sugar free.
Fat free.
Gluten free.
Preservative free.
Carbohydrate free.
Salt free
Genetically modified free.....

You know what?   I just like plain old free!

Kate, my secretary, finally decided that she had had enough. She had had enough of the very long-winded dictation that I kept providing her with. "Dr. K.," she said. "Don't you think you could make your dictations just a bit shorter?" I told her, "No." The reason being that the government had been looking into doctors' notes to make sure that they were of sufficient length and complexity. "I know that," said Kate. "But is it really necessary to document the times that patients bring you free cabbages from their gardens?" Indeed, she was probably correct, but it seemed like such a nice thing to do. I felt like it should be noted somewhere, lest I forget. "What if the government finds out that you have been accepting free cabbages? You could get into big trouble. They could say that you are double billing or playing favorites with your patients."

She had a point. The cabbage sat on the floor of my office in a plastic grocery bag, bulbous and juicy. I looked at it guiltily. It would make a fine plate of coleslaw that would go nicely with some barbequed chicken. If I accepted this particular gift, I was sure that I would be breaching some government rule regarding the fair treatment of patients. Even worse, I had documented these numerous infractions in the patients' charts. I had received green beans, grapes, and a whole host of other edible things from kindly patients who believed that I needed to be fed.

I imagined the headlines in our local newspaper: "Doctor Facing Investigation: Two Tier Medicine For Those Who Garden and For Those Who Don't." This article would contain a picture of elderly patients attempting to grow eggplants on their balconies in hopes of getting faster medical service. They would call my office and advise my secretary they had rather fresh cucumbers that needed to be dropped off really soon, and therefore a quick appointment at the office would be necessary. Some would probably bring a few extra cuc's in their pockets as a casual bribe for my secretary. She also had a weak spot for things organic.

Local farmers would, I am sure, deny that this type of thing was taking place. "No, no. We are just being neighborly. We like to share our produce with friends. The doctor happens to like fresh vegetables. Is it our fault that we have to get in a bit sooner than other patients in order to drop the vegetables off?" Some of the elderly farmers would probably get together on Saturday afternoons to play euchre and chuckle over vegetable stories. "You should have seen the doc's eyes light up when I showed him those tomatoes. They were organically grown and picked that morning, I told him." There might even be a bit of horse-trading going on. "My doctor hates broccoli but goes for Brussels sprouts. I can trade you a head of broccoli for dozen sprouts. I need them quick, as I have to go to the doctor. My blood pressure medicine has almost run out."

Facing my next locavoran offering, I realized the ethical quandary that I and so many other doctors face. If we accept these fruits and vegetables graciously, government and professional bodies might censure us. If we reject these offerings, we must accept lower-quality, imported vegetables from the grocery store.

I tossed the cabbage back and forth, debating what to do with it. Its voluptuous cabbagy aroma and firmness taunting me. What would I do with it if I didn't eat it? I wasn't quite sure what to do. At last, I felt that the most reasonable thing to do was to call a rather erudite colleague to seek some advice. "Hello, Laura," I said. "I have got a bit of a problem. You see, I have this rather lovely cabbage." "Steve, I don't have any recipes for coleslaw, but you can probably make up some really nice cabbage rolls. I'll give you my mum's recipe." "No, no. I just don't know if I should have accepted it. I might be breaking one of those government or medical college rules about accepting payments."

Laura advised me that she would happily destroy the evidence of my misadventure and provide me with a nice tray of cabbage rolls. If I froze them, they would stay good for decades. I stared at the cabbage. Its cryogenic fate awaited; a rather sad fate for such a fresh vegetable.

After dropping off the cabbage to my colleague, I remembered I had already told my wife that I would be bringing home a nice cabbage for some coleslaw. There would be some disappointment with its absence. Vegetables were a way of life at our house.

I debated telling my wife the truth about the cabbage. She would be disappointed and even unhappier at the thought of not getting any more fresh vegetables from patients. She had come to enjoy this small reward that, in a tiny way, made up for the fact that we did not live in the big city. I could imagine her at that moment attempting to convince our children that coleslaw actually was something that they might like. She probably had our daughters mixing up the dressing for it.

Alas, I finally arrived home. "What happened to the cabbage Steve?" I told my wife that it was a long story but my nearest reckoning was that it was getting made into cabbage rolls for use in the event of a nuclear ice age. She wasn't happy.

The next day, I remained perplexed as to what to do with future vegetable offerings. I felt that there must be a rule so that I could at least keep some of the vegetables. Ruminating, I called my accountant, who was a rather slick and clever Toronto guy. He listened carefully and finally told me that he would figure something out so that I could keep at least some of the veggies. He said to me, "Steve, just issue the patients a receipt for the vegetable and send a copy of the receipt to me." I told him that I didn't know about receipts for vegetables. He finally paused for a moment and said, "OK. Don't worry about it. This is what we'll do. Send about half of the fresh vegetables directly to me and I will send them in to the Canadian Tax Office." He paused for a long minute. Then he laughed really hard into the telephone and finally said, "Hey, if it makes you feel better, why don't you just compost more. It's a way to give something back. You can think of it as paying taxes to mother nature!"

I have composted ever since!

—m—

"Do you have insurance or will you be scoring this on the street?"

THE CAT SCANNER

Dogmatic – a special type of revolver used only by police dogs.
PET Scanner – A special type of x-ray done only on pets.
Catatonic – A liquid tonic for cats.
Medicine show – a presentation (consisting mainly of bullshit)
put on by a doctor.
Politician – someone who will do or say anything.

Does any of this make sense?

"OK, Dr. Steve. What's this big plan of yours?" I was sitting with the mayor at his office, trying to figure out how to pay for the CAT scanner that the hospital wanted to purchase. The neighboring hospital, which was about one-and-a-half hours away, had just acquired one that was able to offer ultra thinly sliced pictures of the human body. They were so thin, they were thin as a wafer thus allowing the doctors to find all sorts of unknown lesions that they had no idea what to do with. We were jealous of this. We wanted to find our own incidentalomas that we could spend hours trying to explain to worried patients. The trouble was that the hospital had no money, and the Ontario government also had no money. Even if they had any money, we were quite sure they wouldn't give us any of it. They had other priorities, such as creating more health-care programs with cool-sounding names like Family Health Networks and e-Doc. No one ever quite understood what all of these programs were but there was a rumor that they were secret Internet dating sites for unattached doctors and nurses.

Our hospital needed money from some governmental group. My colleagues decided that someone should approach the municipal government. Rumor had it that they were flush with cash. We didn't exactly know how this was the case. Maybe there were oil revenues from fracking or some sort of pipeline planned? The mayor was an old and somewhat greasy businessman who apparently did some cattle farming on the side (probably as a cover for his fracking and pipelineing). I arranged to meet the mayor at his office, which had been built around 1950 and was replete with his picture on the wall. In the picture, he was wearing some sort of metal mayoral sash. He liked his sash. I sat down in front of him in the leatherette chair. "Welcome, doctor. It's nice of you to come and visit. Do you have an idea for the hospital?"

"Well, sir, we desperately need to get the CAT scanner for the hospital. My plan is to use it on patients during the day and rent it out to local veterinarians at night. They can start using it on animals—you know, like dogs and other pets." The mayor thought that this was amusing. "Uh, Steve. Who ever heard of using a CAT scanner on a dog anyway? Everyone knows cats don't get along with dogs." The mayor was rumored to not be that sharp, so I ignored this remark. "You see, sir, if you help us get the machine, we can rent out the scanner and our radiologist during the evenings. The extra income will help defray the cost to the hospital." "Steve, there aren't that many people willing to spend a lot of money on their dog, even if it gets along with cats." "I beg to differ," I said. "I think we will be able to get a lot of extra cash. They are doing this in other areas of the country, like Calgary (a wealthy oil town out west)." This got his attention. It was time to pull out all of the stops. "And let's not forget about the cows!"

The mayor eyed me with a look of genuine bewilderment. "Cows?" "Yeah, sir. We can scan cows!"

The coupe de grâce came when I suggested that we should start scanning cows to determine if they had Mad Cow Disease. I had envisaged local roast beef containing stamps that said, "CAT scanned and certified free of mad cow." "You know that disease that began when they were feeding the cows with sheep parts? The sheep had been fed cow parts before that, and the cows before that had somehow been fed...Well, I don't exactly know, but whatever it was, it just wasn't that good. With a CAT scan, you can prove that the cow doesn't have Mad Cow Disease." "You want to scan a cow?" "Not the whole cow, stupid—just the head." "But Steve, we don't eat the head—at least I don't, anyway." "Yeah but you can actually tell if the whole cow is sick by scanning the head." The mayor had lost track of everything and was confused. He began rambling. Maybe he had been drinking. His face lit up after he thought for a moment. "Wait a second, doc. What about head cheese. Vern, what is that stuff anyway?" Vern, his oily, cigarette-smoking sycophant, came into the office. He was a short, greasy-haired man with a comb-over. He wore a checkered sport coat and white shoes. "Actually, boss, I think head cheese does come from a cow's head." The mayor turned to me. "You know, doc, I don't think there is a big market for pre-scanned head cheese, but maybe we can look into it." The mayor sat down. He was obviously getting tired of this meeting. The details were too much for him.

"Let me sum this up then, Doctor Steve. You want the town to put some money up for a scanner that will scan cows for cheese?" "No. No sir. The hospital will use the scanner on people." "Wait a minute! What about the head cheese, doc?" asked Vern. I was getting caught in the retard crossfire. "Uh. Look, gentlemen, maybe we can talk about this idea again sometime when I can show you some pictures. "Yeah doc," said Vern. "I would really like to see all the different types of head cheese. I hear that they got good types out in Qweebek." The mayor always liked to have the last word. "Well doc, thanks for stopping by. We'll come by your office and learn some more about the, uh, head cheese and any other meat products you guys want to talk about. Ain't that right, Vern?" "Absolutely, doc. Head cheese: the next white meat—that's my motto!"

I left the mayor's office and picked up some tofu hotdogs. At least I wouldn't have to X-ray them. Hmm. Did they make tofu head cheese? I realized at that point I had to eat healthy. There wouldn't be a CAT scanner any time soon.

—m—

HELPFUL TIP FROM DR K........

Lets say you have been watching a TV show or movie about biker gangs. Don't ever refer to your wife as your 'old lady'. She will probably hit you. Even if she really is an old lady, it will still hurt.

THE RENOVATION

About forty thousand years ago someone decided to paint the interior walls of a cave in Cantabria, Spain. Cave paintings that are several thousand years old have been found all over the world, including North America. No one really knows why this artwork was done.
We might conclude that ancient man had an inherent desire to be creative. Perhaps he wanted to reproduce those animals and scenes that he had seen while hunting. Or... it might have been the guy's wife telling him:
'Honey, we have to renovate. This place needs sprucing up'.

There are few things more distressing to a doctor than having to move his office. Once, I was faced with this proposition. Alas, my previous landlord, who was a specialist doctor, began to complain about the high cost of electricity (*Hey, I like my air conditioning*), the high cost of water (*I often flush twice*), and the frequent requests to change the office air filter (*I am asthmatic. Cough, cough*). The landlord made the mistake of hinting that the rent might have to go up.

I was faced with a dilemma. I had to either start coughing up mo' money or find another office. My current increase in pay would be taken up by an increase in rent. Thankfully, my secretary was able to find me a nice place quite near my original office. The only problem was that it needed to be renovated. Somewhat to my surprise, the rent for the new place was even less than the rent for my original office. It would seem that physiotherapy or pharmacy landlords appreciate physician tenants much more than cranky specialists who are approaching their retirement. I think that the other professional types like to have family docs around *(If you're the landlord, you never have to wait in the doc's office).*

Unlike most renovation stories, this one isn't all that bad. It wasn't all that bad, of course, because I wasn't *paying* for the renovations. I've always noticed that life is a little rosier when you aren't paying. The landlord was picking up the tab as a way of getting me to sign on for a few years. This allowed my secretary and my office manager wife, to spend endless time talking on the telephone and emailing each other. These two alpha females, imagined that they were actually working, when in fact they were just looking through the Home Depot and Sears online catalogs. The two of them discussed a variety of important office issues, such as their preferences for flooring. Would it be a Berber rug or linoleum? What would the window treatment be? We could get wooden, plastic, thin, thick, horizontal, vertical, or Roman blinds. The color of the walls was another question entirely. This would be beige, kaki, off-white, or teal. They liked teal. *What is teal?*

These problems were sorted out without me. My XY chromosome status ruled out any useful input (except money) in this regard. I thought everything was going well, until my secretary approached me with that look of hers.

"Dr Steve," she said. "You are aware that there is no bathroom, aren't you?"

"What?" I said. "No bathroom!"

"Um, yes. There are two bathrooms down the hall for everyone to use."

"You're joking, right?"

"Uh, no. No bathroom. There is a little closet with a sink in it, but they can't install a bathroom because there is no plumbing and the floor is concrete."

My secretary was starting to look scared. She had, after all, chosen out beautiful window coverings. She had waited for ten years to finally have a chance to get new Roman blinds. The whole double flush thing was coming back to haunt me. There was something about using a public bathroom that I didn't like. Other people had .....touched it. My mother had always insisted that we spread a layer of toilet paper over the seat so that we would avoid any contact with germs. "*Germs are the devil,*" she would say. One time, I left the toilet paper on the seat after I was done. The other docs at the hospital crucified me. Also, with all of the extra paper that this process generates, you have to flush twice.

This had turned into a nightmare of future bowel disease that no amount of fiber could fix. I could feel the pressure in my colon rising exponentially.

"There has to be something that we can do."

"I don't know, doctor. We can ask the contractor."

My secretary approached the contractor with the request to install a toilet in our little closet-cum-bathroom. He was a small crusty-looking fellow with a ball cap, cigarette, and an old radio that seemed to only play Johnny Cash. He looked at us with that expression that surgeons have when someone isn't going to make it through their surgery.

"I don't know, doc. There's a solid concrete floor in there. There ain't no flush-*up* toilets. Can't you use the one down the hall?"

"Uh, no," I said. "I have a condition." I didn't elaborate on my condition. Who really wants to talk about their colon anyway?

"Well, doc, I'll research it on the *internets.*"

"The *internets?*"

"Yeah. There is a website for plumbers, you know." The guy looked at me like I was an idiot. A short while later, a new toilet was installed in my office. This toilet actually flushed upwards using an electric pump. It came with a special attachment called a macerator. This large box, which he had purchased on the *Internets*, did some sort of magic by macerating the toilet bowl contents and pumping them up and out of my office. I surveyed the man's handiwork and found it much to my liking. I realized that as it had been just installed. I would be the first person to use it. I would be christening it, as it were.

Ah, I thought, there was no need to spread the toilet paper over the seat. It was brand new and perfectly clean. It probably had just come out of its package.

I prepared to flush. It flushed and then the macerator kicked in. A low growling sound came out of the macerator machine as it digested and pumped the contents up and out. It practically scared the crap out of me! It surprised me enough that I had to flush twice. This was an automatic reflex. At last, I left the bathroom. I felt much like the master of my domain.

The contractor was still in the office. He tilted his ball cap back a bit.

"Yeah, doc, the machine, the macerator, makes a little noise, doesn't it?"

"Yeah, I guess so. Um," I said. "When did you notice the noise?"

"Just a few minutes before you went in there."

The man smiled as his cigarette dangled again from his lip. He was cleaning up his many tools from the floor of the office.

"Yeah, doc. You might say I warmed things up in there for you!"

—·—

"Your heart rate is accelerated, your blood pressure is high, and your hair is falling out. I want you to avoid all work-place related decisions for two weeks."

IN PRAISE OF OLDER WOMEN
(IN WHITE DRESSES)

*Have you ever wondered what men and women really fantasize
about? That's the thing about fantasies. They can really be
about anything. Sitting around in an Operating Room gives
you the time necessary to create vivid fantasies. One of my
fantasies is to play the manly role in someone else's romantic
dream world. The idea here is that it would be neat if someone
actually fantasized about a middle aged, out of shape doctor
(who somehow looks like Fabio).*

*The problem with fantasies is that they can be a little
embarrassing when people inadvertently figure out what kind
of story you are really cooking up....*

Nigella, the Food Network star, was looking at me from
the corner of her eyes. She smiled that warm, broad
smile with her full red lips. She was wearing an elegant
dress that was cut rather low. I could see cleavage. It was
really hard not to stare. She just smiled innocently and
said, "Stevie, I hope you're hungry because you're going
to have something just luscious..."

"Dr. K., wake up!" Whoa. I had fallen asleep in the
ophthalmology room again. This happened to me routine-
ly around two o'clock, when the coffee I had consumed
in the morning wore off. The inactivity in the eye-surgery
room invariably caused me to fall asleep, even though
the chairs were quite uncomfortable. "I saw that smile
on your face. You were fantasizing about Nigella again,

weren't you?" The nurse I was working with harbored a grudge against Nigella Lawson, the Food Network star. She thought that Nigella was a rather pedestrian chef. This didn't seem to matter very much to me, although I did not know why. "If you are going to daydream like that, at least fantasize about a *real* woman instead of that chubby English tart!"

"Actually, I was just resting my eyes for a moment while I considered what new type of needles we will be purchasing—the sharp pointy ones or the dull and painful ones." I am quite sure that no one believed me. There really is nothing like a middle-aged nurse snapping you back into reality. I advised her that my rather rich fantasy life had no real women—let alone real hospital staff members—in it. I also pointed out the difference between chubby and voluptuous.

Like most of the nursing staff, this nurse had a slim and athletic body, which she kept in tip-top form with non-fat yogurt, salad lunches, and endless visits to the gym where she did Pilates, yoga, cross training and, quite possibly, Thai kick boxing. After getting a well-paying job and achieving a slim, attractive figure, I think that it galled her to hear men fantasizing about voluptuous women who serve deep-fried chocolate bars on TV. "Dr. K., anyone who serves fried peanut butter and banana sandwiches shouldn't be a fantasy. She should be your nightmare! Anyway, I have a job for you, as you don't seem to be doing much of anything right now, other than dreaming about your next heart attack." I was about to protest. Then she advised me that I was going to educate a young, impressionable nursing student and that she would be keeping her eye on me.

The hospital where I work had a long-standing relationship with the local community college. This renowned institution had been training nurses for many years, and it had a good relationship with our staff. Periodically, the hospital was filled with young nursing students with eager smiles and fashionable hospital attire. They would follow their instructors through the hospital corridors, nodding and recording facts.

As chance would have it, these students often found themselves in the OR and the recovery room, learning the many new and interesting facts about operative nursing. While everyone likes teaching, the harried nursing staff at our hospital was often unable to do much instructing. This was largely due to the curmudgeonly surgeons placing demands on them. On a busy afternoon, they would typically invite the impressionable young student to "sit beside the anesthetist. He can explain what's going on."

Thus prepared for my new job that afternoon, the nursing student arrived with a quiet knock on the OR door. Her name was Lisa. She looked nervous and was wearing the standard OR greens, which fit her rather snugly. I proceeded to chat her up with the idea of helping her become more comfortable in the OR environment. I explained some things about the anesthesia machine and cataract surgery. It was easy to explain, as I knew almost nothing about these things anyway. Lisa looked considerably older than some of the other students. Most of them were probably under the age of twenty. "Yes, doctor, I am twenty-eight. I was working before I got into nursing." This surprised me and we spent the next half-hour getting to know each other.

In between cases, I invited Lisa to the OR staff lounge and introduced her to the gang. Most of the doctors and nurses were sitting around comparing low-fat, low-carb paleo muffins that looked like dinosaur turds *(note the dino turd - paleo connection)*. One other nurse was explaining how she had used her new juice extractor to make onion juice. Apparently, it was good for battling cellulite. None of the doctors asked whether you were supposed to drink it, apply it to the skin, or use it rectally. We were too afraid that she would try it on us. Sitting down and drinking coffee, we waited for our next case. I happened to notice that Lisa bore a striking resemblance to the actress Sandra Bullock. I commented on this and she blushed. "Everyone says that about me, but you know, she's so much better looking than me." Lisa had that self-depreciating charm that made her even more attractive. I found out that she rather liked cooking shows on the Food Network, and she was a big fan of *Emeril Live*, which was also one of my favorites.

I was really enjoying my afternoon, and I wasn't even tired. "By the way, Lisa, what did you do before nursing school? Were you a highly paid film actress?" Lisa blushed again and told me that she was a registered massage therapist. She had to change jobs because she was getting repetitive strain syndrome in her arms, and she wanted a job with more responsibility. "No kidding," I said. "I've never met a massage therapist, but I send patients to them all the time!"

I went on to tell Lisa about the terrible pain in my lower back. It had been brought on, no doubt, by the cheap hospital OR chairs, which were so completely uncomfortable. I was showing her the point in my back where I had the most discomfort, when she suggested that perhaps my muscles were in a bit of a knot. "How do I get them unknotted?" "Well, I suppose I could have a look at them." Lisa leaned in to me and proceeded to palpate my various back muscle groups, and she quickly isolated the problem area. She then started to massage this area and the surrounding muscle groups while holding me in a slightly flexed and rotated position. In my many years of working, I have never felt so comfortable. I was hypnotized by her slow repetitive stroking and her light floral perfume. I was about to fall into a completely relaxed stupor.

"What the hell is going on here? Get your hands off of him! You were supposed to be instructing her on operating room techniques—not fooling around like this!" The head nurse had seen Lisa and had come up behind us. She looked at us with eyes that were daggers, her anger radiating from her swollen red face like some sort of negative energy aura. "Uh, did Lisa mention that she was a licensed massage therapist? She was just showing me some of the therapy." I was trying to sound professional, but the surgeon was snickering in the background. The apoplectic head nurse turned to Lisa and said, "You have wasted enough time with 'La-Z-Boy' over here. Come with me and I will show you how to operate a gas sterilizer. In fact, there are a whole bunch of things I'd like to sterilize around here!" With that, she left the room with the nursing student and a look that could kill small rodents. I think I squeaked like a little mouse as she left.

When the next batch of new students came around a few days later, I noticed that I was pointedly not asked to supervise them in the OR. Oh well. It was time to get back to the crossword puzzle. *What is a four-letter word for a waste product that rhymes with* misfit?

—ꙮ—

"You'd already know how I'm feeling if you
had read my blog."

THE NEW WING

Peanut butter and Jelly

Peas and Carrots

Coffee and Doughnuts

Champagne and Caviar.

Money and Power

Sex and Money

Black Nylons and Stiletto Heels

You know where this is going. Don't you......?

"Who is this Dr. Adam Richardson, anyway?" Tony, the general surgeon, was asking me who the new chronic care wing was named after. The 'Dr. Adam Richardson Memorial Wing' was soon to be completed, and its completion would be celebrated with the requisite fanfare from the politicians, hospital administration staff, and boundless supplies of coffee and mini doughnuts. "I don't know, Tony. It's funny that we haven't heard of him. He is a doctor, though." Most of the elderly doctors who had begun their careers at our hospital were, in fact, still living. The hospital was erected in 1950. The legendary surgeon who did its first operation was finally put to pasture only a few years ago. He had been confused but he still felt game to operate. A picture with his distinguished countenance, which was lined with years of experience and hard work, graced the hospital's main corridor.

We are often reminded that the first surgical procedure that was completed at our institution was a circumcision. For a while, the snickering anesthesia staff expressed a desire to become a 'center of excellence' in circumcision, but like so many of our efforts, this fell by the wayside. Apparently, some pediatricians in 1970s thought that circumcision was inhumane. Ironically, we later learned that the lowly circumcision procedure actually lowered the chance of men becoming infected with various diseases, including AIDS. Tony, the surgeon I was working with, was one of the old guard who continued to work despite being over sixty-five years of age. He could often be heard cursing Nortel under his breath. This organization and his children's rather expensive education were largely responsible for his continued presence on the hospital call roster.

"Steve, as the head of your department, I want you to find out about this guy they are naming the hospital wing after." I reminded him that I was extremely busy providing anesthesia for his patients, and I said that he could call the head of surgery to obtain this information. "That prick doesn't know anything, Steve. I always see you chatting up the managers. Find out for me, OK?" Tony and many of the other doctors had noticed that I had been getting cozy with the various hospital managers, and they treated me with veiled distrust. This in no way stopped him from making outrageous demands on me that were irrelevant to my job as an anesthetist. However, like so many anesthetists, I had a compromising and somewhat

lackadaisical attitude toward life. I merely nodded my ac-
quiescence to him over the *Newspaper* crossword puzzle.

There was more to his request than just idle curiosity.
I had moved from Toronto to the small town where I was
currently working. The surgeon I was working with was
quite different. He was born and bred in the same small
town where he was currently working. I think he half-ex-
pected the new wing to be named after him. He seemed
somewhat miffed at the name of the new wing: The Doctor
Adam Richardson Chronic Care Wing "OK, Tony. I'll make
some calls and see who this mystery doc is."

I called a variety of doctors and found that none of
them knew who this doctor was. Finally, having spoken to
numerous staff members, I was told to track down an older Czechoslovakian internist who had retired and moved
to Toronto. I had worked with him for a few years prior to
his departure. I called his home and got a hold of his wife,
who said, "Yes, hello. My husband is out today, but you
can reach him at 787-7426." She seemed rather cryptic. I
had really expected her to be a bit happier with her retirement. I called the number and got him on the phone.

"Da. Dr. Krause."

"Dr. Krause? It's me, Steve. You remember me from
Community Memorial? How are you?"

"Steve," said Dr. Krause. "It's you! It's nice to hear from you."

"Uh, did you just say *da*?"

He went on to explain that he was now working at a
clinic for Russian immigrants. "I thought you were retired," I said. He replied that since the Nortel meltdown,
his Retirement Investments had tanked and he had to either work or starve. "Toronto is an expensive town, you
know. By the way, who is managing your investments,
Steve?" I told him that it was a broker whom one of the
Emergency physicians had recommended to me. "Holy

[*Russian expletive*]. That's the same prick who turned my retirement into a living hell. Get rid of him!" I asked him about Doctor Adam Richardson, whom the new hospital wing was to be named after. He didn't know any one by that name, except for maybe a dentist. He also gave me the name of a retired KGB operative who had recently immigrated to Canada. The KGB man, he said, could "fix my investment advisor for a few rubles." I declined this graciously, reasoning that whoever replaced him would be even less competent.

Getting nowhere in my search for the identity of the wealthy benefactor, I finally confronted the director of the Hospital Foundation. A very attractive woman in her thirties named Buffy O'Driscoll ran the foundation. The Hospital Foundation was the organization that accepted charitable donations on behalf of the hospital. Buffy's perfect makeup and hair, along with her four-hundred-dollar shoes identified her as an alpha female. She had mastered the art of ego-stroking wealthy elderly gentlemen out of their vast fortunes.

"Why are you so interested in the new wing, Steve. Do you want to make a donation?" the foundation director asked. She then licked her lips, crossed her legs, and fixed me with her best come-hither look.

"Uh, no," I said. "I really don't have any money right now." Nor would I have any money for a long time, based on my investment advisor's performance. Silently cursing that I had forgotten to get the name of the Russian hit man, I quickly changed the subject and asked how the new hospital wing had received its name.

"That is a very interesting story, Steve." The director then told me that a few months ago, a rather wealthy elderly gentleman had contacted her about making a sizable donation to the Hospital Foundation. When she met the man, she realized that the donation was really quite sizable. "Actually Steve I was really very impressed."

"He made a really big donation, did he?" I asked.

"No," she said. "Noooooo...... Steve, it was really, <u>really</u> big. Then it got bigger! And it was *hard!*"

"Hard?"

"Hard cash," she said. "Some people try to donate soft assets; he donated very hard currency. Then he donated some even harder currency – gold. Can you believe it?"

The foundation director licked her smooth red lips again and smiled, remembering her latest conquest. "I had several meetings and he took me out to diner a few times. I realized that he was so much more than generous. After his exquisite offer, we really had no other choice but to name the new wing after him," she said. The Foundation Director went on to mention that Dr Richardson drove a blue Porsche and was a scratch golfer at the local Golf club. "Basically Steve, Adam is a wonderful philanthropist and one of the most successful men in this community. He's a retired dentist"

The guy wasn't even a medical doctor! The only time he ever went in to the hospital was when he had hurt his back – presumably while lifting his gold bullion out of his Porsche! The jerk had made a vast fortune on technology stocks. He was lucky enough (or smart enough) to pull his money out just before the market had collapsed. The gold he had amassed from people's teeth probably!

"You know, I am hoping some of the staff doctors who are nearing retirement will make contributions like Dr. Richardson did. It really is great that you can be remembered on such a grand scale after you retire."

"Whoa," I said. "You mean to tell me that a wealthy *dentist* who has had absolutely nothing to do with this institution is now going to have a new wing named after him?" I was flabbergasted. "Couldn't you have named something else after him, like an elevator or maybe a toilet?"

Later that week, I met up with Tony and gave him the awful truth. "Jeez, Steve. Those damn dentists always come out on top. By the way, what was the name of that Russian guy Krause told you about? I have to make a phone call."

The doctor's investment strategy:
Catch a falling knife and put it in your pocket.......
Then tell your friends who are doctors to join in!

—∞—

"Don't ask me about the side effects. I've never taken this stuff."

THE FLU QUIZ ARE YOU READY?

A lot of concerned people have approached me recently about the upcoming flu epidemic. Actually, we are not entirely sure if this is an epidemic, a pandemic, or just a crafty media-demic that has been designed to foster concern and better news ratings. Be that as it may, we Canadians are a well-traveled lot. We like to go to all sorts of locations, and we bring back souvenirs from our travels, such as SARS, hepatitis, head lice and bad tattoos. The question remains, however: how will we cope with the upcoming epidemic? As an altruistic doctor, I have come up with a questionnaire that might help readers prepare for the big day, when some worried-looking expert comes on television saying, "We are concerned, *but don't panic.*"

Read on. Educate yourself on the coming maelstrom with this short questionnaire.

Question #1
You see two people standing on a corner, and they have their elbows out and their hands on their hips. They seem to be touching each other's elbows. You don't know what you are witnessing, and you are wondering if you should join them. What do you do?

1. You assume that this is some sort of Toronto gay pride thing, and you quietly back off.

2. Realizing that you have just seen the new Toronto-style handshake, you offer up your elbow just to be friendly.

3. If you're from out west and have always harbored a grudge against Toronto, then you quickly kick one of the guys in the crotch while his elbows are out. Then say 'that's the new Calgary handshake. Just trying to be friendly!'

4. Sneer a lot. Then give everyone the finger and say, "whatayoulookinat eh"? Trust me, people will just figure you're a local Toronto resident.

Question #2

You have been invited to an office dinner party. You have to go, as your boss insists that it will show team spirit. Barfing and crapping together bring people closer like nothing else – especially when the office has only one bathroom. The dinner party is supposed to be at one of those all-you-can-eat buffet restaurants. The company pays for the whole thing. You are deeply conflicted. Your general porcine nature is in conflict with the fear that you might get the flu. What do you do?

1. Show up at the restaurant, sniffling and looking kind of sweaty. Mention to everyone that you took a cab over and that the Asian driver sneezed on you. Your office coworkers will suggest that you sit at a separate table or possibly in the bathroom. Quietly sneak out. They won't want you to come back to work for weeks.

2. Make sure your insurance is paid up, and then go crazy at the all-you-can-eat seafood bar. For good measure, wash the meal down with a nice dose of Ribavirin and some Echinacea.

3. If you have made up your mind that you are going to eat something at the buffet, at least avoid a few

dangerous foods. Avoid chicken because it might be contaminated with salmonella. It's also better to avoid beef because of mad cow disease. Also, you had better avoid anything raw from the salad bar. Come to think of it, you should also avoid fish, as it might contain too much mercury. That leaves bread sticks. Wash this down with a delicious bottle of spring water.

4. Alcohol is a good disinfectant. Use it wisely and use it often.

Question #3

You have arrived at the office, where there is now a mandatory flu vaccine clinic. The nurse has a trolley filled with painful-looking syringes. She says that she has one just for you. You hate needles. What do you do?

1. Wink at the nurse, turn around, pull down you pants, and say, "Let's make this quick." This will likely leave her and your coworkers aghast. In the confusion resulting from your mooning someone and being charged with sexual harassment, everyone will forget that you never actually got your shot.
2. Act quite eager to have your shot, but at the last moment mention that you developed a terrible rash and passed out the last time you had a flu vaccine. Ask the nurse sweetly if she knows CPR.
3. If you absolutely have to have a vaccine, scream really loudly as you get it and say, "Jeez that hurts. Did you just stab me with a fork?" Then pretend that you have to get a blood transfusion and take the rest of the week off.
4. See if you can download a waiver from your lawyer stating that if you get sick from the vaccine, the

nurse will be held responsible. She will avoid you
like you already have the flu.

Question #4

Most people have to go to the doctor every once in a while.
Usually, this is quite harmless. It's usually associated
with a lengthy stay in the waiting room and an all-too-
brief visit to the MD. We all know that doctors' offices are
cesspools of infection. They are too crowded and everyone
there has either got a cough, a cold, or something else
nasty like farty diarrhea. What do you do?

1. Cleverly demand to be the first patient of the day,
   thus avoiding any new germs. You will only have to
   put up with the germs that were left in the office
   from the day before. Tuberculosis can live a long
   time in a doc's office.
2. Bring your own can of Lysol and spray everything
   in the office that you might come into contact with
   your body. Let's hope the doc doesn't have to do a
   rectal exam.
3. Even though you might get away without touching
   anything, you will still be susceptible to airborne
   contaminants. You can avoid this by not breathing.
   Yoga might be good for this.
4. If you think about it, the safest way to avoid airborne flu particles is to take up smoking. By only
   inhaling through a lit cigarette, you will automatically be sterilizing the air with fire. Try not
   to think about the fact that you will be robbing
   yourself of oxygen. At least it will be germ free.
   Additionally, people will give you lots of personal
   space.

Question #5

Like every other nut job, I attempted to get some anti-flu medicine, but I found that drug stores do not carry it. The pharmacist tells you that the government has halted the sale of it, and it is stockpiling it in some secret vault. It is supposed to be released in the event of a flu outbreak. What do you do?

1. Relax and feel safe in the knowledge that your government has got things safely under control, just like when we had SARS.
2. Hit eBay. Hopefully someone has got some Tamiflu for sale. Pray that some Jackass doctor from Ontario won't outbid you.
3. Join a political party quick! Maybe you can get a job in the government. No one has any idea just how this medicine is going to be distributed once the outbreak happens. Most docs believe that after the families, friends, coworkers, families of coworkers, friends of coworkers, and rock star friends of the politicians have been given their doses, there might be some left for the rest of us to fight over.
4. Stock up on beer, pretzels, American Idol videos, and Johnny Cash records, and stay out of sight until the whole thing blows over (2020).

Hey, I hope this questionnaire has helped you prepare for that awful day when even going to the doctor seems like a bad idea. Take it from me: it is a bad idea – and my office will probably be closed.

—〜〜—

HELPFUL TIP FROM DR K.........

If you are going to ask me for ED (erectile dysfunction) pills, don't be a 'fraidy' cat and wait till the last moment when I'm about to leave.

And don't ask for free samples.
What do you think this is? Halloween!

GOOD AND BAD NEWS....

*You really can't hold a good man down. Although I started out
as an unwilling participant in the hospital administrative seen,
I became more and more drawn to it. Like Darth Vader, Michael
Corleone and all of those other tragic figures, I started out well
intentioned but was ultimately sucked in to a deep dark abyss.
This whole thing was fueled by the usual culprits – Crackberry,
caffeine and cheap carbs...*

Coffee, low fat muffin and trusty lap-top in hand. I had
finally mastered the art of holding a departmental
meeting. This was relatively easy, as there were only five
of us in the department. My main goal with these meetings
was to get the holiday time and weekends that I wanted
off. The truth was that I usually didn't care all that much,
but my wife always had something important planned,
such as a trip to see her parents. I therefore studious-
ly planned and deliberated over the schedule, carefully
placing myself on call when my in-laws visited. I was also
on call during the weekends our family spent antiquing,
furniture shopping and visiting The Pottery Barn. The
whole thing was actually working out quite well. I had
not seen my mother-in-law for over a year. I was also well
on my way toward getting better chairs for the Operating
Rooms. During our operating room committee meetings, I
had developed a technique based a shark feeding frenzy I
had seen on National Geographic. The idea was to get one
surgical group fighting with another and then sit quietly

by as they wasted the hour-long meeting hurling insults at each other. This kind of constant infighting, I found, achieves a sort of stability that is reminiscent of the US Congress.

Like any good thing, there always has to be something that threatens to disrupt the smooth, orderly functioning—or non-functioning, in this case—of my life. This came about when we learned that the young ER doc who had just finished his MBA had decided that he didn't want to be the Chief of Staff. Instead, he decided to go to work for Doctor's Without Borders. The nerve of the guy! He probably figured that the working conditions within that organization were way better than at Community Memorial. He was obviously one of those Gen-Y slackers who think that life's supposed to mean something. *Idiot!*

The news of this clever young fellow abandoning us hit the staff like a ton of bricks. It felt like we had been rejected by eHarmony. This never happens, does it? Without the new young chief of staff, the hospital management was now looking for anyone to fill the vacancy. The only person they could find who was gullible enough to take the job was a semiretired pathologist who was the head of the operating room committee. All of the various surgeons and anesthetists sat on this committee. It was also the only committee I had to attend as a representative of the department of anesthesia. I liked the old pathologist because he didn't talk too loudly. He was so quiet that people sometimes thought that he was dead. The lingering smell of formaldehyde and his very low respiratory rate kept the meetings rather subdued. His medical experience largely involved looking after lab specimens, and he thus had little to say about any living patients. He was the ideal head of the operating room committee;

unfortunately, he was so good that the administration now wanted him to be the Chief of Staff.

The hospital management pointed out that during his entire career, he had never actually had any disagreements with patients, and he had never had a complaint registered against him. Dead people tend to not do that sort of thing. The hospital administration felt like this was an advantage, as he had a very clean record. He was a very good second choice to the young, good-looking emergency doctor with the MBA who now was probably part of a documentary called "Canadian Doctor Shortage: Why? They're all in Africa!" Once again, my anesthesia colleagues approached me about how these momentous happenings would affect me. Barry, my colleague finally spoke to me.

"Steve, the guys have been wondering about how things are going with you being the department head? By the way, I've noticed that you have started wearing glasses. What's with that?"

"Things are going well, Barry. I feel I've really settled into the whole thing, especially the OR committee. During the last meeting, the surgeons started throwing muffins at each other! The glasses are from the ophthalmologists; they're safety glasses. I don't want to get caught in the crossfire and get a raisin in the eye."

"Oh, well. As you know, there will be some changes. The current head of the OR committee, Dr. Faber, is going to be moving into the chief of staff position."

"Oh, that's great for him. I think he likes going to meetings, but sometimes he sits so still. I don't think he's breathing. Um maybe his pacemaker needs to be dialed up? Does he have a last will and testament?"

"There's a problem, Steve. They need a new head of the OR committee, as Faber is leaving. This is called succession planning—promoting the guy you hate the least to be the boss."

"Yeah, I figure they are going to have to look around and find one of the surgeons to do it."

"That's the problem, Steve; the bone docs don't like the general surgeons, who don't like the urologist, who in turn don't like the gynecologist."

"That's OK," I said. "Just get the bone guy then."

"Actually, *all* of the other surgeons don't like the bone doctors! That just leaves you. I'm afraid that you will be voted in as the next head of the operating room committee."

"What the hell! You promised me that all I would have to do is be the head of our own department. Now you want me to be the head of the entire operating room committee. It's a big committee. Those people are scary! Half the time, they say they're going to *cut* me."

"I know you're just joking, Steve."

"Actually, one of them showed me the knife he was going to use if I crossed him. He keeps it in his briefcase for special occasions."

Barry just smiled and said to me, "Stevie, what you need to do is camouflage yourself."

"But how?"

"I don't know," he said. "Pretend you're a low-fat muffin?"

Around this time, I decided to pursue a Masters in Business Administration (MBA) . I am not entirely sure why I enrolled. In truth, I thought it would be entertaining. It was kind of like how some people find the running of the bulls in Pamplona Spain entertaining.

—◊—

"The doctor will see you shortly. Try not to disappoint him"

THE RESEARCH PROJECT

" We are followers—not true scientific leaders. Although we do quite a lot of follow-up research, it is clear to me that we should really be trying to do some unique ground-breaking work. This study I have outlined is completely original, and it will clearly benefit medical science—possibly even mankind itself..."

I was addressing the Medical Advisory Committee (MAC). This committee was the big important hospital committee that all of the department heads were a part of. I was pitching a new study that I was trying to do. The study involved monitoring anesthesia-department comfort levels against patient satisfaction. Having tried unsuccessfully to get the hospital to fund the purchase of new La-Z-Boy recliners for my department, I had hit upon the idea of doing a study. The advantage of doing this was that part of the study costs would include the leasing of the new OR chairs. This purchase would cost nothing for the hospital.

A guy in my MBA class told me that the federal government might dole out some cash for new industrial research, and I knew that using anesthetists to rate various chairs might actually provide the chair designers with some scientific and ergonomic input. We were given a small grant, and I had planned to lease a few chairs from a local La-Z-Boy gallery. I had rather cleverly worked out the lease arrangement for the chairs. Once the study was completed, the store could then supposedly donate the chairs to the hospital for a sizable tax deduction. It was a win-win scenario, I thought to myself. This was why I went to business school. It was such a brilliant plan that I thought I would write it up as a case report for the *Harvard Business Review*.

I had to gain hospital approval to do the study. This involved giving presentations to both the Medical Advisory Committee (MAC) and the Ethics Committee. So far, the MAC had not given me a hard time. I had threatened to whine unbearably and not approve anything for anyone else until they allowed my study to proceed. I had privately polled most of the other committee members and told them to kiss their new equipment goodbye unless they could guarantee full cooperation. One of the other department heads had the gall to ask me if the study was ethical, and he implied that the only reason I was doing the study was to get new chairs for my department. Replete with a button-down shirt, a bow tie, and glasses, he was one of those intellectual, internal-medicine type doctors.

Intellectual doctors are the bane of ordinary stiffs like myself. I knew that the logical thing to do would be to present my study proposal directly to him and have him review it with an eye for 'evidence-based' medical conclusions. Knowing that he would find some sort of criticism, I did not do this. Instead, I went to his department at 7 p.m. and replaced all of his nicer office chairs with the old OR chairs. The next day, I sat by the telephone, reclining in his faux-leather executive chair and waiting for him to figure out what had happened. Intellectual types never really understand the Michael Corleones of the world. It took his department a few days to locate their chairs. His secretary then delivered a hastily written note, in which he offered his assurance that his department would approve the study. Word got around about my thievery, and various departments began putting stickers on the chairs that loudly proclaimed, "PROPERTY OF INTERNAL MEDICINE DEPARTMENT: DO NOT REMOVE."

I introduced the Medical Advisory Committee to the study through a brief memo. I was sure that some of the other doctors would be envious of this new study. Unlike the cholesterol pill mega-trials that were already going on at the hospital, I was planning new original research. I imagined that someday my research would become part of some scientific breakthrough. The study involved measuring some physiological (blood pressure and heart rate) and psychological elements through a questionnaire. It was with the psychological profiling of both the patient and the anesthetist that I hoped to develop a better understanding of people under stress. This part of the study would broaden the scope and also provide me with a chance to get a Nobel Peace Prize, as well as the Nobel Prize for Physiology and Medicine. I began to walk around in a John Nash kind of haze, mumbling scientific formulas and theorems. I did this to convince my colleagues of the genuine belief that I had about the project. I had even worked out a snappy name for the study. It was officially dubbed the LADDERS project. It stood for Local Anesthesia Department Doctors Ergonomic Study.

The Medical Advisory Committee presentation went well, and I was reassured that after the department members reviewed it, they would approve it at next month's meeting. I was hoping for immediate approval, but there did not seem to be any chance that this would happen. In this regard, the hospital moved ponderously slowly. This was no one's fault; it was just that doctors behaved like a herd of cats. All of them moved in different directions, except when they smelled something fishy. With me, something always seemed to smell fishy.

A month later, I was full of anticipation at getting the go-ahead for the project. I had made a point of being particularly nasty to those who had previously denied me my new OR chairs. I had made small signs with adhesive backings to stick to the chairs, advising the OR staff that the chairs were "for study-use only." The sign also said, "Users are required to wear undergarments at all times."

The Medical Advisory Committee meeting droned on and on. The CEO was going on about this committee report and that committee report. Finally, we got to the business of my project. I was relieved. Years of study, effort, planning, and blackmail had gone into this moment, and I finally felt that the recognition I deserved would come. Most of the department heads raised their hands to approve the plan; however, two guys didn't. I eyed them maliciously. They were smiling.

One of the dissenters spoke up and said, "Mister chairman, we in the department of medicine feel that the study fulfills the minimal requirements for approval, but we believe that the name should be changed to more accurately reflect the nature of the study. We therefore approve of the study under the name Chronic Recurrent Anesthetic Pain Study—that's CRAPS, for short." He said the word 'craps' a little too loudly, and he went on to mention that the new name "kind of had a ring to it." Not to be outdone, the head of orthopedics mentioned that his department had thought long and hard about the study—a whole two minutes, I figured. They had also come up with a much better name for the study. They suggested calling it the Lumbar Anesthetic Recurrent Disk Disease And Sciatica Study. "That's the LARDD-ASS project, Steve." We figured it would make a great study for publication in the *New England Journal of Furniture and Upholstery*. With that, he and the rest of the group began laughing uncontrollably.

When I arrived at the OR the next day, my new chair had arrived. Someone had stuck a note to it that said, "Do not touch—belongs to LARDD-ASS."

Can't anything ever be easy?

—⚞—

THE RESEARCH PROJECT PART 2

Study Log Entry, Day 14:

Having spent the past month deeply involved in my clinical trial, the preliminary results seem positive. I have noticed a more relaxed and buoyant mood among my staffers, and the ridicule I have suffered at the hands of the surgical staff have finally subsided. My study of the relationship between the anesthetist's level of comfort and the patient's level of satisfaction has shown promising results. They are, in fact, so promising that the second arm of the study, in which the older and more decrepit OR chairs are brought back for a month, may not even be necessary. I liken this to that study on Coumadin (blood thinners), in which the study was abandoned because the results were obvious and it was just too dangerous to go on.

After designing and executing a brilliantly designed and executed study, you would think that a doctor would catch a little respect, but alas this 'looked for graciousness' on the part of others was found to be wanting. In this respect, a certain surgical team was especially unscrupulous. The team of urologists seemed particularly envious of my study chairs. They spent every possible minute lounging in the chairs and making phone calls home and ordering pizza for lunch. Most of them claimed to be quite gassy as soon as they stood up. They often advised me that they had warmed the chairs up for me. One guy even planted himself in the chair and asked one of the nurses if she would like to sit on his lap. She politely refused.

Like any doctor pretending to be a genius, I merely overlooked these slights and adopted a Deepak Chopra-like sense of calm. I kept saying things like, "I understand you are probably not fulfilled in your life. Perhaps you need more spiritual time." I would say this while sitting comfortably on the La-Z-Boy chair with the footrest up and my Birkenstocks comfortably slipped off.

I happened to notice an unusual phenomenon. It seemed that the calmer and more relaxed I got, the more agitated the rest of the surgical staff became. I had to keep telling them to breathe. I tried to tell them in a very slow and deliberate way, "Just breathe." At first, the nurses just smiled at each other. After we were called in at 7 p.m. to do an appendectomy, though, a nurse named Loretta glared at me and finally lost it. She hissed, "Don't you *'breeeeethe* me, you eastern, mystic, doughnut-eating fake! I'm missing my weekly yoga and potluck night, and we were supposed to have a visiting instructor from Toronto. The instructor actually *met* Woody Harrelson at that University of Toronto yoga class during the Toronto Film Festival." She went on to say that this instructor had actually taught Woody and it was a real honor to get invited to his class.

Thankfully, the case ended quickly, though it took some extra time for the surgeon to find the rather normal-looking appendix. This allowed the annoyed nurse to catch the last half of her yoga class. I mentioned that it was probably a vegan-only event. I offered to let her take some of the moldy, dry fruit that had been sitting in the OR lounge fridge so that she would fit in better at the potluck that her yoga class was holding later on that evening. She declined this, mentioning that gourmet tofu hotdogs from British Columbia were in her car already. Loretta looked at me rather queerly in my Birkenstock sandals and said, "I know it's just killing you to check out this yoga class and our visiting instructor. Why don't you come along with me?" The truth was that I wasn't that interested in the class; I was more interested in the free potluck dinner, as I had nothing to eat at home and didn't feel like eating at a restaurant.

I did not have any appropriate yoga attire, so I kept wearing my OR greens and Birkenstocks. I went to the class hoping that I wouldn't actually have to do any real yoga before I could get my free dinner. I figured that if it was all vegetarian, I could stop on the way home and pick up some bacon somewhere. When we arrived at the class, I was surprised to find that it was in the basement of an old church. There was a table in the foyer with numerous crock-Pots filled with lentil-based vegetarian dishes. We entered a classroom. The hushed crowd was listening to the instructor while seated in the full-lotus position. I quickly sat down cross legged on a hospital towel I had brought and made like everyone else. I sat at the back so that I would be close to the food. Mercifully, the class ended after ten minutes. My stiff knee joints were grateful. The instructor thanked the class and we filed out quietly. Ah, I thought. Free dinner!

During the dinner, we were all encouraged to grab a plate and help ourselves. I was a little disappointed that there was no beer or wine. I guess that sort of thing wasn't allowed. I had to make some small talk, and I found myself chatting up a middle-aged woman who was positively ecstatic about the visiting instructor, as if he were a rock star or something. "Oh, wasn't the yogi just wonderful?" she said. "He was so calm and centered." "Yeah, I know," said I. "These fried things are pretty good. What are they?" Just at that moment, the visiting instructor, Julian, came up to us and asked if we had enjoyed the class. "Er yeah. It was great. Some good moves and stuff." I was trying not to eat too fast. "I noticed you are wearing OR greens. Are you a doctor?" "Actually, I am. I was just completing some emergency surgery, and we had to hurry so that I could make your class." I figured a little buttering up wouldn't hurt.

For some reason, the yoga instructor seemed to want to talk. So, I told him about my cool new research project on perioperative stress. He seemed impressed. I also suggested that the hospital was supposed to be getting OR greens made out of hemp, but they had "sold out to the man." Due to cost cutting, the hospital had gotten the cheaper, polyester cotton-blend ones. When I told him this, he looked rather sad. Then he nodded and said, "I hear you, bro." The instructor didn't seem to mind that I was a total beginner. We chatted for a while about various tofu recipes. It was then that I noticed that Loretta was giving me a funny look. I figured that she was probably mad at me, as I was there only to scarf down some free food. The rest of the class probably wanted to talk to the instructor far more than I did. Before I left, Julian made a point of shaking my hand and thanking me for coming. "Maybe I'll see you again at the class, Steve." "Uh yeah," I said. "I hope so."

In the parking lot, I finally caught up to Loretta. "Ha!" I said triumphantly. "Who's the doughnut-eating fake mystic now?" I had to rub it in just a little bit. "Don't be so smug, Stevie," she said. "You were talking up the instructor so much that the whole class thought you were queer!"

"Oh."

Loretta smiled at me and said slowly, "Just breathe baby—just breathe."

HELPFUL TIP FROM DR K.........

If by chance your cell phone goes off while I am attending you in my office. **Do not answer the phone!**
**If my cell phone goes off ...... wait! I don't carry one
at work.**

THE TEST

"Help! I can't breathe. Cough, cough. Wheeze" That's what I tried to say, but no sound came out. Oxygen levels dropping. Losing consciousness. Couldn't breathe, and I was sure the Grim Reaper was coming for me. Strange what you think about in these moments. I was hoping my underwear were clean, and I wondered how long it would take for my body to be found. This was all that I could think about. Nausea was overwhelming me and I was about to wretch up my morning coffee and low-fat carrot muffin. Everything was going dark. With my consciousness fading, I saw a tunnel of light, and I swam toward it.
OK, OK. I didn't really see the tunnel of light but you get my drift.

I was in the infection control office undergoing a test to see if the surgical mask that the hospital supplied would protect patients from my germ-laden breath. "It's for your own personal safety, Steve. You don't want to get SARS when you treat someone, do you?" The infection-control nurse sounded so reasonable on the phone that I decided not resist coming in for the mask test. I could not have foreseen the nasty surprise that was waiting for me on the third floor of the hospital.

The problem had begun many months ago. There was a short news clip on CNN that showed a venerable medical institution in Toronto attempting to deal with the SARS outbreak (SARS stands for Severe Adult Respiratory Syndrome). Unfortunately, the clip featured some guy in OR greens standing outside with a mask half on his face smoking a cigarette. The implication was that the clean operating room you might be having you're surgery in might be contaminated by some downtown Toronto filth. There was also an underlying message to US viewers: don't get sick in Toronto, unless you want a smoking guy to operate on you.

The public and the hospital administration saw this example, and many others, as exemplifying our laxity with infection control. The CEO gave the heretofore unassuming and quiet infection control people large responsibilities to "clean up our filthy hospital." The hospital board, eager to show the public their understanding and concern for infection control, readily approved this action. Mainly, they didn't want to look like the mayor of Toronto, who thought the World Health Organization (WHO) was an English rock band.

After a lengthy discussion at our medical advisory meeting, the infection control group was charged with new hefty portfolios to control the spread of disease. We discovered at the meeting that our current surgical mask would not protect a particular doctor with a large Grizzly Adams beard. Sporting a snappy Euro-style goatee, I really didn't care, but I did feel sorry for this fellow, whom they pointedly told to trim his facial hair. I thought they went too far when they also said that he should get a hair cut—his hair style was a bit 1970s—or get a hair net.

"It is very important that you wash your hands before and after you handle the appliances." The infection control people kept referring to the surgical masks as respiratory protective appliances. They passed them around, handling them with great care. I was struck by how large and hard they were. They were unlike the flat wrap-around masks that I was used to. They had some sort of flap on the front, and they looked very much like a jock strap. I kept the one that they were passing out, figuring that I could use it as jock protection for my next hockey game. I reasoned that they were strong enough to keep my privates protected and germ free. They also smelled a great deal fresher than my current jock strap.

After several weeks of increased infection surveillance, we began to notice that the heretofore meek and humble infection control people had morphed into a pint-sized group of Machiavellian dictators. They strutted around wearing armbands and began issuing a wide variety of edicts. They even placed a letterbox in the staff lounge, whereby staff members could rat on others if they were caught not washing their hands. Also, they came in and inspected the OR techniques to ensure appropriate sterility.

I first noticed them as I was walking into the OR room, holding a cup of coffee in one hand and a newspaper in the other. I had a Boston Crème in my mouth, doggy style. The infection control nurse glared at me and asked, "Dr. K., why are you bringing food into the OR?" Caught red-handed, I thought that I would try and brazen it out. "I thought that it was OK to eat food in the OR, so long as I bought the food at the cafeteria. It's sterile, isn't it?" The nurse looked at me for a moment. I could tell she was trying to decide whether I was serious, stupid, or just seriously stupid. "Look, at least the coffee ought to be OK. It's boiling hot."

"Remove yourself and that doughnut from the Operating Room right now!" The nurse made a note on her clipboard and walked out glaring at me. "I told the team leader that you should also change your OR greens before you go back to work, as you have spilled coffee or something on them." I felt like I should say that at least I wear undergarments under my greens, but I couldn't talk. My mouth was full.

Days later, a notice was put up instructing all staff members, especially the OR staff members, to get mask tests. Failure to comply with the test would result in the cancellation of OR time. The team leader nurse mentioned that the infection control people would have to approve of the new OR recliner chairs that I had requested. I felt that I had to get on their good side.

"Ah yes, the doughnut doc. Well, the test is really quite an easy one." The balding and somewhat overweight infectious disease specialist said. He told me that all I had to do was put on the mask. He would then put some sort of plastic barrier over my head and spray some test material around. If I didn't smell anything, I would pass. He looked at my stylish goatee, shook his head, and said, "Hmm. I don't know." I tried to smile. Then I squashed the mask on tightly and made exaggerated breathing movements. Much to my surprise, he then put a large bag over my head and began spraying something into the bag. For a moment, I thought he looked a bit evil—like he was going to enjoy the whole nasty spectacle. I should have realized that these lab doctors always have it in for cool heroic types like myself. It was then that I noticed that he was spraying not just some test material but something that smelled like the essence of garlic-eating, sweaty, fat-guy armpit.

The stench was unbearable but under the mask I seemed to need to hyperventilate because the airflow resistance from the mask was so great. I mumbled, "I can't breathe." I began to wheeze. It was then that I began to have my near death experience.

Later that morning....

'Take some slow deep breaths," the ER doc said. Thank god. I was back in the land of the living. "Don't give me that cheap generic stuff. I want real name-brand drugs!" After calling a code blue, I was whisked off to the ER, where a very young ER doc who looked like she was seventeen years old attended to me. "I just got off the phone from the Infectious Disease specialist who gave you your mask test." I was angry. "The nerve of that guy—giving me a full-blown asthma attack!" "Actually, Steve, we think you just had a panic attack. You weren't that wheezy. You seemed to get better once we got you to slow down your breathing and gave you an Ativan." "Panic attack? I don't get panic attacks!" She rolled her eyes. "Whatever, Steve. Anyway, he said you just passed the test, but he recommended that you shave your beard and change your OR greens before you go back to work. Oh and there's no eating in the ER. I noticed you uh, sometimes bring doughnuts in here. OK?"

I didn't shave and I didn't change my greens and I still eat doughnuts and low-fat carrot muffins. They leave a pleasant, nutty taste whenever you throw them up.

—m—

HELPFUL TIP FROM DR K.........

If your wife keeps bothering you about leaving the toilet seat up, say to her 'Honey I think my prostate is acting up'. The only problem is that she will ultimately force you to get a prostate exam.
(That's the one where I say 'bend over')

THE STAGES OF ONE'S LIFE

"Daddy, look – I've made a new type of chocolate cake. It's got rum in it. Oh by the way, could I have a few friends over on Friday night."

"Well princess, that cake looks really nice. What's the occasion?"

"I just thought I would do something special for you dad. So.... can I have a few friends over?"

"Well, its okay with me, just make sure you ask your mother."

(Said while eating chocolate rum cake)

Having reached the exalted age of forty-five, I had come to believe that most of the traumatic stages of my life were behind me. I had finished medical school. I had gotten married and witnessed the births of my three children. Though my wife claims that I slept through her labor, I was awake for the delivery. The only thing left was to cruise into early retirement, play golf, show up at my kids' weddings, and check into a nice nursing home, right?

Sadly, this was simply not the case. My plans for an orderly life of working and leisure were derailed last week, when my sixteen-year-old daughter announced that she wanted to have a small get-together with the numerous friends she corresponded with on something called Facebook.

Now, every family has its own internal dynamic. I had always thought that my children loved and respected their dad. They were extra loving and respectful when they needed something like money or new stylish clothes from Abercrombie and Fitch. Things, however, took on a whole new dynamic when my youngest child reached the exalted age of sixteen. Overnight, my sweet little over-achiever went from being the champ at the science fair to a social butterfly. No more microscopes, nature studies, and piano lessons; instead, she spent a whole lot of time now on skin, hair, and nail care.

When change comes about, we all react differently. Understanding the social needs of our children, my wife reinvented herself as the cool mom. I, however, became surlier. I developed a fondness for telling my children that I could support an entire African village on the money that they spend on their social activities.

Things finally came to a head one day when my daughter announced that she wanted to have a small get-together involving twenty of her closest friends. I had to ask her how anyone could have twenty close friends. She told me that it took a lot of hard work to maintain these friendships. This explained her mediocre school perfor-mance. My daughter did not want my wife or I around when these people were at our house; however, I insisted on being around then. What were we supposed to do? Were we supposed to go to a hotel? I was thus able to wit-ness the whole teenage party in all of its sordid details. About ten scruffy-looking boys wearing ball caps and ten squealing, giggling girls wearing very low-cut blue jeans and push-up bras descended upon my house.

I won't bore you with the details. For example, they somehow snuck alcohol into my house and managed to steal my alcohol after they ran out of their own. The low point of the whole ordeal was when several of the young ladies vomited in my front hall, in the bathroom, and in the kitchen.

In the interest of helping others, I have come up with some observations about drunken teen behavior. I know that this particular area of research does not lend itself to the randomized double-blind trial; however, I fancy myself somewhat of a scientist. Having never been published in any sort of scientific journal (the back page of the *MedPost* is as scientific as I get), I will offer my own observations and conclusions to those facing similar circumstances. Perhaps others who have gone before me might also confirm the veracity of these *bon mot.*

Helpful tips when trying to understand drunken teenagers:

1. The easiest way to understand a drunken teenage boy is to simply go to a zoo and spend some time observing a troop of baboons. They eat and scratch themselves. When opportunities arise, they copulate. You could probably get a bunch of baboons to wear ball caps, though I've never tried this.
2. Teenage boys have seized upon the idea that forty-year-old cool moms are all cougars looking for sixteen-year-old guys who wear ball caps and scratch themselves. In order to get the attention of said forty-year-old female, they will often take their shirts off and scratch themselves some more.
3. Young girls tend to drink more than young boys. This allows the young boys to then take advantage of the gin-soaked females. Sex ain't the half of it. The latest fad is to take pictures with cell phones and post them on Facebook.
4. Teenagers have bought into that whole management concept of not asking for permission for

something. Rather, they assume things are OK until you say that they aren't. Case in point: your twelve-year-old scotch isn't for them to share with their friends because, as they will say, "Like, sharing is good, isn't it dad?"

5. As with Jane Goodall and other primate researchers, one must at some level communicate with the group that they are studying. Dr Phil says, communication is very important. Learn the lingo. *Hotastic* means a girl who is inclined to be friendlier than others, *while drunk.*

6. When all else fails and things are wildly out of hand, just call the cops. Yes, I know that the embarrassment of having one or possibly three police cruisers show up at your house is rather much. The advantage, however, is that a police report might be helpful when you make an insurance claim for that piece of furniture that was accidentally set on fire.

Remember, these are just stages that families go through. Someday, you will all get together and laugh at the fond memories. I personally will laugh the hardest at the memory of a mouthy, shirtless punk getting tasered and dragged off to the drunk tank. His shirt came in handy for cleaning up the vomit.

—∞—

"I don't do much traditional exercise. But I make sure to get my heart rate up by freaking out at the office on a regular basis."

YOU LOOK GOOD IN GREEN

Business School Instructor:
"Remember people, the real goal here is to always aim for a win-win scenario."
"What exactly does that mean professor?"
"I think that a win-win scenario is that mythical arrangement whereby both you and I—but mainly I—get something out of a particular arrangement".
(Cost of an MBA – roughly $100,000)

<u>October 10, 2012. 07:00</u>

Oy-vey. I was caught in operating room committee meeting this morning. Thankfully, I have my Blackberry, a cappuccino, and some breath mints. The low-fat cappuccino and the Altoids are from home, as the hospital is now too cheap to supply appropriate early-morning nutritional supplements. They say that this is due to budgetary reductions. The funny thing is that these same budgetary restrictions don't ever apply to things like the senior executives taking leave to attend conferences or board members attending pricey ribbon-cutting ceremonies. The latest problem was that we were spending too much money on OR greens. The management believed that someone was stealing them. The manager actually gave me 'the look' when she said this. I think she was implying that maybe I was taking them. Did she have inside information? It may have been that website I visited, which was

called, "How to Sell Surplus Hospital Equipment in Iran."
It was supported by the AOE (Axis of Evil) Network.

"Does anyone have any ideas about how to recover the
missing OR greens?"
I remembered that in Kingston they posted a newspaper
add that depicted the OR staff seminude with a note asking people to return their gowns. I raised my hand eagerly.
"Lets take some nude photos!" In retrospect, maybe
this didn't come out quite the right way.
"Dr. K., for once in your life can you move on from the
hooligan nude photo thing."
The nursing staff seemed rather confused with my
suggestion, except for the one male nursing student with
the barbwire tattoo on his arm. He smiled at me earnestly
and said, "Cool, man. My place or yours?" I didn't answer
him. The manager said, "Look, people, we have lost a lot
of OR greens, and if we don't get them back I am going to
bring in our security consultant."

October 14, 2012. 07:30. A Special Meeting with a Security
Consultant

The security consultant looked like an over-the-hill
ex-cop. He is a heavyset, beefy fellow. He doesn't smile.
He has that pissed off expression that men get after they
have been divorced several times. He likely took this security job to pay for alimony.
"Now look, people, my previous job was to find and
prosecute welfare fraud. I brought over three hundred welfare fraud cases to justice. I am going to get your uniforms
back and prosecute the culprit, if it's the last thing I do."
He thumps the table, causing a small tidal wave in my cappuccino. *Holy sh—! Dirty Harry over there means business!*
I immediately started formulating plans to return the
OR greens that I had used when I painted my deck. Wait a

minute. What if he does some sort of CSI thing and figures out that the stains are from my deck? I look around to see if anyone else has a guilty facial expression. Everyone else looks a bit uneasy. The rest of the gang probably had decks to paint also. I make a play at misdirection.

"Uh, yeah," I say. "I think a bunch of skateboarding hooligans are coming in after hours and stealing the greens." The security guy looks at me. "Skateboarding hooligans?"

"Yeah. Skateboarding hooligans. They are the kind of punks who grow up and try to defraud welfare." Hearing this, I see the man's jaw tighten up. He says nothing and we file out of the room looking guilty.

<u>October 16, 2012. 09:27. In OR #2, (with surgeon performing a hernia repair).</u>

The headline in the local newspaper, the *Intelligencia*, which should be renamed the *Stupidia*, says, "Hospital Security Official Suffers Heart Attack at Skateboard Park." Apparently, our security consultant had confronted a couple of skateboarders who were wearing Gap khaki pants. After chasing them on their skateboards, he passed out, having suffered a coronary. The skateboarder was quoted as saying, "Yeah, the old dude wanted our pants and I said, 'Like, no way, man. Are you gay or what?' Then he, like, grabbed his chest and then passed out. So, we tried to resuscitate him with our iPods by playing some really bad-ass tunes really loud in his ears, but it didn't work. Then my mom came and called the ambulance."

Oh well. Do you need something to wear while painting your deck?

THE DINNER EXTRAVAGANZA

*With their limited middle-class jobs and humdrum lives, I often
wonder how my parents ever managed to raise two successful
children. I think it's a Canadian story that really illustrates our
country's greatness. You can come to Canada or America with
nothing in your pocket, and through hard work you can come
out on top. Of course, the opposite is also true. You can spend all
sorts of money on your kids and have very little to show for it...*

Does anyone like January? This is the time of year
when there just isn't anything really great going
on unless you have the cash to go to Mexico or to the
Caribbean. Thanks to my new gas-guzzling truck, I did
not have this kind of money. I figured that if I couldn't
go somewhere warm, I might as well contribute to global
warming with another V8 engine.

I have often wondered why some women prefer to marry
doctors, as opposed to people in other perfectly respect-
able trades. Many of these people, such as plumbers and
electricians, actually work in very lucrative trades. One of
the reasons why doctors are so popular is because of the
Annual Hospital Gala. Plumbers and electricians don't
have ridiculously expensive galas. A hospital fundraising
committee ran our gala. Typically, the dinner costs about
two hundred dollars. For this two hundred-dollar dinner,
I would get some crusty bread rolls, a salad, and a main
course. A local celebrity chef prepared it, and it was usually chicken. *It would seem that everyone is a celebrity*

*chef these days; however, the only celebrity chef that I
know who cooks chicken goes by the title of 'Colonel'.* Now,
two hundred dollars is a lot of money for a meal, but that
ain't the end of it. My wife typically has to get her hair
and nails done. She has to get a new dress and possibly
new shoes or a handbag.

I was thus about five hundred dollars lighter as I sat
down at the table with my colleagues and their wives
in the elegantly decorated hall where the function was
put on. The committee had hired a string quartet, and
the MC of the night was none other than Mr. Smarmy
Perfection, the hospital chairman. There he was, dressed
in a tuxedo. He was smooth as an oil slick, chatting up
the local rich folk. I had noticed that there were doctors
arriving in their Toyotas and dentists arriving in their
BMWs. Thankfully, none of the other women at the table
wore the same dress as my wife. If this were to happen to two guys, we would nod at each other and mention that we must have got our tuxedoes at the same
joint. Women don't like to look the same; maybe they
figure we'll compare how each of them fills out the dress.
My wife and I were seated with the boring middle-aged
group. Jean liked this group largely because the other
women had children and thus could be trusted to not
look significantly better than her.

As the dinner began, the wine began to flow. What
unfolded before me was an episode of *Degrassi: The
Soccer Mom Years.* The women began to talk about their
children—how bright and gifted they were. I made the
observation that there seemed to be a lot of supposedly
gifted children, but I rarely ever met a truly gifted adult.
Somehow along the way, most people seem to lose their
'gift' and become rather boring and stupid. My wife gave
me a rather caustic look when I offered this comment,

and she mentioned that our daughter had recently won the gold medal at the local science fair.

One of the ladies, Joanne, said, "Yes, I saw that your daughter Elizabeth won the science fair with her project. What was it called again? 'Bacterial Contamination of Vegetables and How to Control It.'" That was a very sophisticated project that your fifteen-year-old daughter did." Joanne eyed me like a mom who has noticed a few crumbs around the cookie jar. I had to respond. "Hey, man, all I did was taste the vegetables and tell her they all tasted like vinegar. It was her mother who helped her with that project."

There was a sudden hush at the table, as the other women cast accusing glances at us. My wife, Jean, was quick to explain that she had merely helped our daughter with getting the vegetables and explaining how to culture the various foods and grow the bacteria. It had been my daughter's idea to spray the vegetables with a vinegar solution to see if this might get rid of the bacteria. Joanne didn't seem to be buying this explanation. She elaborated.

"Well, my daughter's project only got an honorable mention."

Jean was interested in this. "Oh really. That's quite good. What was it on?"

"It was called 'You're in Trouble with Urine Trouble.'"

"Oh, and what was the project about?"

Joanne elaborated. "Oh, it was about the development of drug-resistant bacteria in people's urine."

Making a mental note of the fact that Joanne's husband was a bladder specialist, I said, "Hmm. You must have been quite *pissed* off."

The other ladies at the table were not going to be outdone. They each went around the table talking about their children and just how wonderful they were. I learned that

Joanne's daughter not only did science fair but was also a champion lacrosse player who was soon to be heading to the Olympics. The other woman, Shelly, calmly told us that her daughter was recently accepted as a page for the House of Commons. Finally, the last lady, who was younger than the rest of them, had a toddler who was learning the piano and had just learned to play *Moonlight Sonata*.

I wasn't quite sure what happened to my wife, but I think she finally snapped. For years, she had been trying unsuccessfully to one-up the other ladies. This had led her to spend more and more time on fruitless piano lessons, ballet lessons, and for a while horse-whispering lessons. I could have purchased another child with all of the money I had spent upgrading my current ones. My wife's efforts had resulted in three very demanding kids who spent a lot of time e-mailing friends and playing Xbox.

I have never met a woman who didn't believe that her offspring were somehow superior. My wife had just been reminded that there were other special children who were perhaps even more special than her own. Faced with reality, she did what any normal mother would do; she concocted an elaborate lie..

"Well, Greg, our son has recently started his own business." This involved selling alcohol to his friends. It was a profitable enterprise, but it involved selling _my_ alcohol at a 100 percent profit. I therefore had to put an end to it. My wife kept at it. "Oh yes, and our older daughter has started filming her first documentary video." This was a documentary about a girl who gets a bad hairdo before the high school prom and winds up shaving her hair off. *Yes, my older daughter shaved her head bald, but we drew the line at her getting a tattoo.*

At last, the end of the dinner drew near. We had been given our requisite black forest cake and coffee. My friend, the bladder specialist, turned to me and said, "So, Stevie, that was quite an ordinary meal for two hundred bucks. Are you coming next year?"

"Probably not."

"Why not?"

"I'll be too busy helping my gifted children get into college."

"Your job will be to provide this practice with the appearance of medical expertise."

THINGS FAMILY DOCTORS LIKE

OK, OK, OK. Enough with the patting yourself on the back! Everyone knows that the Canadian health-care system is the envy of all sorts of Americans. They wish they had universal coverage. They wish they had lower costs. They wish they had tort reform. They wish they had better access to generic medicine. It's a matter of fact, Canada is probably the one destination that most Americans would head to if they couldn't live in the US. All the same TV channels, fast food outlets, and strong beer, what's not to like about Canada?

Michael Moore has been schlepping around Canada for a while. When a few Canadians who were voicing their dissatisfaction with the health-care system confronted him, he told them to quit whining. I liked it when he said this. I liked it a lot.

This prompted me to come up with a list of things that Canadian family doctors like. Everyone is different but lets face it, we are all part of some cohort group that has been studied and categorized by demographic specialists. Do you think that you are the only doc who secretly likes Yellow Tail Shiraz? Put down that glass and guess again!

Now, there are always going to be a few docs out there who will pretend that this list is quite inaccurate. The thing is that I've developed this list not just by interviewing Family Doctors. I compiled this list with the assistance of a bunch of disgruntled bone doctors, general surgeons, and pediatricians who happen to be married to family docs! You can run, but you can't hide.

Things that Canadian Family Doctors Like:

1. Patients with carefully printed out medication lists. This helps you because your brand new office computer system has got you so confused that you now only use the system to watch YouTube and play Sudoku (while the patients are talking).
2. Healthy young people who only come once a year to receive a combination flu shot, annual medical exam, and smoking-cessation counseling.
3. Christmas presents with alcohol in them. The counseling that you have given over the past several years on the advantages of red wine is now bearing handsome rewards. I used to recycle the brandy-filled chocolates, but last year my teenage daughter found them.
4. Gullible specialists who can be flattered into taking your ninety-seven-year-old demented hospital patient. Typically, what I do is look through the old hospital chart until I find some cardiologist consultation note from back in 1974. Most likely, the cardiologist who saw that patient is still alive - and working.
5. Family docs like having their evenings off. This is family medicine we're talking about. Emergencies are for ER specialists—and surgeons, internists, anesthetists, and nurse practitioners (and anyone else I can think of).
6. We really like medical education events in Las Vegas or—even better—on a luxury cruise ship.

'Oh, that lecture on glaucoma was so fascinating'!, Especially after a few glasses of Yellow Tail Shiraz.

7. Colonoscopies. Hey, everyone is getting this done: Big movie stars, family members of movie stars, patients who have friends of friends who have relatives who had cancer. I've even got a couple of general surgeons on speed dial. They even offer patients a free video – of what, I really don't want to know.

8. Pharmacists. They are a great resource when you just don't feel like talking to people. They can spend hours talking about the potential side effects of their medicines to people. This typically causes the patients to reject their prostate medicine in favor of saw palmetto. It's natural and therefore can't have any side effects.

9. Family Doctors also like to redefine themselves by taking up other activities. I'm a doctor but my real interest is whitewater kayaking or going to Michael Buble concerts. Oh, and lets not forget - drinking Yellow Tail Shiraz.

10. Those Cholesterol pill samples. You can only go so far with your diet, oatmeal, and an elliptical machine. Whatever happened to those minoxidil samples? (Not that I need any—they're for a friend!).

OK, not everyone likes the Yellow Tail Shiraz; some of you prefer Wolf Blass. Be true to thine own self. Get off that YouTube website and book yourself an educational course on a cruise ship. Some of them offer wine-tasting and Italian-cooking classes. They might even offer colonoscopies.

For those of you who aren't family doctors, remember this list at Christmas time, and don't look at my computer while you're in the office!

—∭—

A CHRISTMAS STORY – AND WHY CHINESE RESTAURANTS REMIND ME OF THE HOLIDAYS

"Steve, Christmas has to be special this year. You have to get more into the spirit of things—no grumbling or complaining. Everything has to be perfect." My wife had that crazed look in her eye. You know the look. Women always get it when they find a new shoe store. It's a combination of pure excitement and squealy pleasure.

I consider Christmas to be a nice time of year. I try to think about all of the good things that one should concentrate on, such as conveying goodwill to my fellow man. Charity, family, some carols, and maybe getting a few days off of work also helps. The thing with any family is that with the passage of time things change. My three children no longer get dressed up in little suits and fancy dresses. They no longer become excited with decorating the Christmas tree or wrapping up gifts for each other. Back from university, they now descend on my house with bags of dirty laundry and demands to borrow my car. When they aren't eating and leaving dirty dishes around, they are in their rooms. They are on the Internet doing something important like updating their Facebook profile or Skyping with their genius boyfriends.

In my house, there are relatively few arguments. They do occur, however, with regularity at Christmas. This usually has to do with presents and gifts. In my day, my folks wouldn't give us many gifts, but they did give us some spending money. They always felt that a guy in college needs a few bucks; my dad referred to this as 'beer money'. The idea of giving our children some money didn't sit too well with my wife. I think that this acknowledged that they were becoming adults. She didn't like this. She therefore bought them expensive presents, like iPads and imported leather boots. After Christmas, I was then stuck with giving them beer money.

I therefore approached Christmas with trepidation. I anticipated a big credit card bill and a whole lot of cleaning and dishwashing in my future.

This past Christmas came around and indeed it was rather special. My son was with a new girlfriend. She had never celebrated Christmas. She was Jewish and would be visiting our house over the holidays.

On hearing this news, I was struck with a feeling of pride. My family would be this young woman's first exposure to Christmas. We were to be 'Christmas ambassadors'. My wife, Jean, gave me very explicit instructions:

1. Offer everyone alcohol but don't drink too much. When she said, "Don't drink too much," she actually meant, "Don't drink anything."
2. Don't let any gasses escape my body, unless I was alone outside.
3. Make sure our dog, Larry, did the same.
4. Try to relax and be myself, but not too weird or embarrassing (How??)

Jean had decided that the dinner on Christmas Eve was to be an extravaganza. She had recently completed a Cordon Bleu chef course, and she was very fond of her chef jacket. It looked like the ones that fancy chefs on TV wear. Every food imaginable was going to be prepared. It was going to be like a meal from *Downton Abbey*.

At last, Christmas Eve arrived and I had followed her instructions very carefully. Even Larry, our dog, had been behaving himself, although I think he was wondering why both of us were spending so much time outside. "Steve, why don't you take everyone for a long walk around the neighborhood while I finish making dinner." I have found that these polite suggestions aren't really suggestions but orders from high above. I therefore politely herded the children and my son's girlfriend out the door for a long walk. This would give Jean an hour or so to finish making a Christmas dinner that was fit for a celebrity chef. We bundled up and walked around, chatting about the weather. I learned that Jewish people often go out for Chinese food on Christmas, as these are often the only restaurants open.

The walk was refreshing and invigorating. The children and I returned to our house cold, hungry, and a little bit excited. We entered the house and I could tell that something was wrong—deeply wrong.

A loud alarm was wailing in the house, and there was smoke in the kitchen.

"Steve, thank God you're back. The candied yams caught on fire and set off the smoke alarm. Quickly, press the button on the alarm system to shut it off!" Every burner on the stove had food on it, and the oven was going like mad with smoke billowing out of it. My wife was in a panic. I dashed to the alarm pad at our door, but I could not figure out how to turn off the alarm. I pressed one of the buttons. It didn't work. I pressed another button and then another. At last, the alarm stopped.

"Phew. That was tough. What's going on?"

"The yams are burned. Everything else is OK, though."

At that moment, the telephone rang. We really didn't want to talk to anyone, as the final touches to the extravagant meal were being finished off. I picked up the phone. A very serious voice came on the line.

"Hello, this is Alarm Systems Management. Did someone just trigger the alarm?"

"Yes," I said. "But it was an accident and it's all over. It was just some burned yams."

"Yes but it seems someone also pushed the intruder alarm."

"I must have triggered that by accident."

"OK, but you have to give us the secret code word before we can close this call."

I asked my wife for the code word. She had recently had the alarm system installed. I handed her the phone. Code words are usually old pet names. I had a sinking feeling.

What followed next was very uncomfortable. Jean took the telephone.

"Hello, I don't remember the code word. Is it Fuzzy?" This was the name of our first dog. She was wrong.

"Is it Honey Bun?" This was the name of our first horse. She was wrong again.

"Is it Shadow Fox?" This was the name of our second horse. She was wrong again.

"Is it Larry?" This was the name of our current dog. She was wrong yet again!

All of the answers were wrong, and we were running out of pet names. Jean was going to have to move on to the name of our hamsters next. Even I could not remember the name of the hamster. She simply could not remember the secret code word.

The Alarm System representative came on the line again and said those dreaded words: "I'm sorry, ma'am. You don't know the code word. I have to send the police. Surrounded by burning food and an out-of-control situation, my wife finally lost it. "Don't send the F—— police!

Don't you realize it's F_____Christmas Eve? This is my home. I am going to report you to your manager!"

Thirty minutes later, not one but two police cruisers arrived at our house. The neighbors were actually staring through their windows, wondering who was going to be arrested: Jean, me, or both of us. I had a sudden urge to go hide in the backyard with Larry our dog. I suppressed this urge.

The first police officer said, "Excuse me, sir, but we got a call from Alarm Systems. The fire and intruder alarms were triggered in your house. We are here to investigate."

The second police officer said, "Yes and apparently someone tried to threaten the Alarm System worker. We have to talk to everyone in the house."

Two hours later, the dinner was cold and the turkey was very dry. The police made everyone line up in the front hall to make sure that there was no domestic situation. They demanded to see everyone's identification, and they questioned everyone, including the children and our guest.

The first police officer said, "Well, madam, you sounded very threatening to the alarm system people. They actually thought this was a domestic assault situation."

"Well, officer, my candied yams were burning."

"That really is no reason to threaten the alarm system people. They are just doing their job. After all, it's Christmas, you know."

Later that evening, I said, "You know, Jean, I think we should do this every Christmas." I was eating chicken balls with a red sauce. The sweet and sour sauce was quite tasty. We had to go to the one place that was open on Christmas: the local Chinese restaurant. My son's girlfriend had suggested this. While we were there, I had to have the last word.

"Yes, Jean, you said that everything was to be perfect this year. And you know it is!"

"How is that, Steve?"

"The chicken ball sauce is red and Christmassy. Also, I wont have to do the dishes afterward."

Since then, I have always tried to go out on Christmas Eve. Alas, I have had no luck. As one last note, don't offer police any alcohol. They really aren't guests and it just doesn't help the situation.

Merry Christmas!

—m—

"Sorry, that was the three cups of coffee, four cans of Red Bull, and double dose of Paxil talking."

MAKING A DEPOSIT AT THE BANK

Future predictions for North American society:

<u>*Cryomancing*</u> – *A new form of internet dating that men engage in that will allow you to impregnate a woman's frozen egg with your frozen sperm in a lab somewhere.*

<u>*Menpathy*</u> – *A weird sort of emotion whereby you feel sorry for some guy. Usually he's trying (unsuccessfully) to cryomance some attractive woman in her 40s.*

<u>*Moneymoon*</u> – *That period of time where you feel like you have done something really clever, like spending thousands of dollars preserving your sperm (that no one wants).*

<u>*Manginapocalypse*</u> - *This is what happens after you realize that your sperm count is too low and therefore not worth preserving anyway.*

Ontario doctors actually agreed overwhelmingly to their new government contract. They knew something the government negotiators didn't know. The week prior to voting in support of the contract, the country's economy tilted toward a deep abyss—the kind that ultimately leads to health-care cutbacks. Not surprisingly, a short while later, we were treated to the news that hospitals were over their budgets and cutbacks needed to be made. The gravy train was over. The idea was that we were all somehow slothful and inefficient. We needed to work more efficiently, like a well oiled government office.

The thing with being in dire financial straights is that it can release some creativity that would otherwise remain dormant within our subconscious minds. This is something like when you are dying of dehydration in the desert and you come up with the idea to drink your own urine. It makes perfect sense; you just didn't have the clarity of thought until that moment.

In such a moment, I found myself sitting with a gynecologist and an urologist the other day. The ob-gyn mentioned to me that he had noticed that many couples seemed to be postponing pregnancy until later in their lives. They did this so that they could get a handle on their careers and financial situation. They might, for example, buy a Lexus and a condo in Florida. The doctor was worried that these couples would probably have fertility problems. The notion here is that as you get older and more decrepit, your eggs and your sperm get older and more decrepit. Freshness counts. This doc was thinking of opening a sperm and egg bank. If you can't have fresh eggs and sperm, then get 'fresh frozen' eggs and sperm. The sperm-and-egg bank would bring in paying customers. We all needed paying customers. The trouble was that we needed at least ten thousand dollars for the necessary cryogenic storage equipment. It seems that you always need money to make money.

Around this time, one of our urologists walked in wearing a smile under his blond frosted hairdo. He announced that he had just gone out to the waiting room and a young woman had blurted out that 'he was so hot'. There is something about urologists. Women love them—or what they stand for, anyway. It was then that I had an epiphany of sorts: "I know, guys. Let's produce a sexy hospital calendar. We'll use the proceeds from the calendar to purchase the equipment for the sperm-and-egg bank. Then we'll use the money from the sperm-and-egg bank to keep the hospital running." The idea made perfect sense to me. I made no sense to anyone else, but even Da Vinci understood that sex could be used to sell anything.

I took my idea to the Hospital Foundation to see if they would help get the idea off the ground and consider paying for a photographer. The CEO of the foundation wasn't a medical type, so I had a lot of explaining to do.

"So, let me get this straight, Steve. You want us to fund a calendar filled with sexy pictures of doctors and nurses. You then want the proceeds of this calendar to purchase equipment for a sperm-and-egg bank that would be located in an unused part of the hospital. The people with deposits in the bank will then pay a monthly fee to keep their 'junk' in storage. We can then give the monthly fees to the hospital to help with their funding." The CEO seemed to grasp the plan fairly quickly.

"Um, Steve, where exactly are they going to collect the eggs and the sperm?" I told her that we could collect the eggs in the OR – it was a minor surgical procedure. All we would need to collect sperm was a room with a bed, some old porno videos, and a sterile plastic cup. As it turned out, our on-call room was already set up for this.

The CEO asked me where I got this whole idea. I told her it was not really an original idea, as one of the nurses had recently been in a calendar for another charity called Granny's for Africa. Her picture was rather sexy, so that technically made her a GILF. "Uh, Steve, do you actually have enough people to pose in this calendar." "Sure, we have lots of DILFs and NILFs." The CEO looked a bit confused. At this juncture, I wasn't even sure what I was talking about.

Alas, the whole wonderful plan fell apart a week later.

As it turned out, the young woman who thought the urologist was so hot turned out to be fifteen years old and mentally challenged. I should have realized this after I found out she was in the hospital to get her teeth cleaned. This didn't bother the urologist all that much, but we realized that his market niche was rather small. The other DILFs and NILFs didn't seem to be all that interested after we told them that the proceeds of their pictures would be used to fund a room in which people would come in and masturbate (the sperm collection room). Some of them mistakenly thought that their pictures would actually be in the room. The last straw turned out to be the cleaning staff. They refused to clean the on-call rooms unless new hand sanitizers were put in and all of the plastic cups and old porno videos were removed. It would seem that the road to financial wellness is long, hard, and quite possibly slippery.

Take it from me; don't tell your DILFs and NILFs why they have to take off their clothes for that group photo you've wanted to take. It's easier to just bribe them with a little Yellow Tail Shiraz and tell them that their pictures are going on your Facebook website if they don't cooperate.

Footnote:
(DILF) Doctor I'd like to be 'friends' with.
(NILF) Nurse I'd like to be 'friends' with.

—◊—

HELPFUL TIP FROM DR K.........

Necking with your boyfriend or girlfriend in my office examining room - not cool.

Eating sandwiches in my office – not cool.

Showing up to my office smelling of weed (and burgers) – not cool.

THE DYNAMIC DUO

The more things change, the more they stay the same. Here I was, once again passing gas for one of the surgeons. The highlight of the day was the youngster, a fifty-one-year-old fellow. The rest were well past their three score ten and two. The surgeon was droning on about how his kids were bankers. "London, Paris, New York," he said. "I tell you, they are traveling all over the world first class." His children's educations had been paid for by the legions of appendices that had exited the hospital in a jar over the past twenty years. I could not turn my laptop on. This left me disgruntled. As a replacement, I opened up a freebee journal—I think it was called the *Journal of Prognostics*. It was free and it had vivid color pictures of nasty, crusty skin lesions. My favorites were the tongue lesions and the 'body piercings gone wrong'. I showed these to my kids.

I was thinking of writing to advise the editors that their journal would be better if it had a sunshine girl and boy—you know, some shiny, smiley-faced type wearing a stethoscope and hopefully nothing else. Then, I spied something interesting. There was a large advertisement from one the pharmaceutical companies. It wasn't your regular ad with a fat guy looking for cholesterol relief. It was about some sort of competition in which the contestants would send in a short story promoting teamwork between pharmacists and doctors. I imagined that it must have been a very profitable year for the US-based multinational company that promoted this—low-priced generic medicine be damned!

The rather novel competition invited applicants to write short stories about how these two professional types worked together. You also had to send in a picture. The prize was an educational grant. If I won, I would spend the grant playing golf at an educational conference in Florida. The prize sounded fairly good and my interest was piqued.

Our little hospital had two part-time pharmacists. Robert was a good-looking fellow who was intelligent and thoughtful, and he dressed sharply. He was probably no older than twenty-seven. The other pharmacist was a woman in her early forties who was from the UK. Her name was Shona. She was quite attractive, and she had a mesmerizing, soft English accent. She looked a bit like Nigela, the Food Network star. The thing with competitions like these was that you had to come up with some sort of novel plan to win the prize. I had a plan.

For years, I had relied on the pharmacist to help me with my geriatric care patients. I would admit them to the hospital and have the pharmacist figure out how much medication or what types of interactions these patients might have. They had become so good at this sort of thing that it was now standard practice to call a pharmacist in to determine the type and amount of medication we should give each patient. I felt that this would be a good reason to enter the contest. Although this alone was a good enough reason to win, I knew that the competition would be tough. We would have to spice up our entry.

"So, you are entering a contest involving doctors and pharmacists?"

"Yes, Shona," I said. "It's going to be great. We could win an educational grant!"

I was trying to win Shona over with my enthusiasm. Shona looked a bit suspicious.

"I don't understand, Steve. Why do we have to pose for the picture in the *nude*?"

"Well, you do want to win, don't you?"

I had concluded that the competition for this little award would get entries from all sorts of health facilities across Canada. This meant that we needed an angle. I had learned from a marketing class at business school that sex sells everything.

"You know, I'm not talking about a full-frontal, John-and-Yoko kind of picture. I'm thinking of a more artsy kind of thing: a black-and-white photo with soft lighting. Maybe both of us would be topless." I was hoping for the kind of thing you might see in *Rolling Stone Magazine*. I had recently purchased a digital camera. This seemed like the ideal time to try it out. We also had a hospital photographer who was anxious to take pictures of things other than ribbon-cutting ceremonies. My main concern was that although Shona was an ideal photo candidate, I was somewhat more than ideal—twenty of thirty pounds more, actually.

After giving it much thought, I came up with the idea that both of us would wear lab coats with nothing underneath. Shona would stand in front of me with her coat unbuttoned, and we would put a caption under the photo that said, "Doctors and Pharmacists at Community Memorial: Nothing Comes Between Us!" The hospital photographer was so excited that she offered to let us use her home studio. As we prepared for the photo shoot, I began to realize that Shona had a splendid figure. I dieted and did sit-ups. At last, we set a date, which I think we both faced with a little trepidation.

There was a bottle of chilled white wine waiting for us at the studio. The place was awash with ethereal music and soft mood lighting that accented Shona's plum-red lipstick. We both disrobed and put on our starched lab coats in the photographer's little changing area. Shona stepped out and I realized that her body was that of a slim Venus. She was all dazzling womanly perfection. She looked at me quite boldly, smiled, and gestured for me to come forward and stand with her front of the camera. At last she spoke, "Its time for you to play Doctor".

With my heart pounding like a teenager, I gently placed my arm around her waist. I could smell the lovely perfume of her chestnut-colored hair. She slowly let the lab coat drift open, and my hand slipped down to her tummy. I pressed her against me while staring at the camera. Her leg slipped out from below her black mini skirt, exposing black fishnet stockings and glossy high heels. She had a luxurious smile on her lips. I was caught up in Shona's intoxicating feminine charm. The photographer stood in front of us by her camera that was on a tripod stand. She calmly encouraged us while the soft music played. The camera clicked and clicked. We touched each other, slowly slipping our hands underneath the clean white fabric. Her skin was like soft silk. The photographer made us do a little dance to some music to help loosen the mood. As we changed our positions here and there, we continued posing until somehow both of us were topless and my hands were atop her shapely breasts. At that point I realized that we couldn't go on any longer – I was getting a little too excited.

Every once in a while, certain people surprise you with their sexiness. It's like a little mystery. We both returned to our very professional roles the next day. I chose the best picture to send out with our application for the award. I accompanied this with a fawning letter advising the company that we used a lot of their various products. I really did think we had the competition in the bag.

Months later, the letter came back from the company. I opened it up eagerly, imagining that it contained a check for a goodly amount of money, which we would judiciously spend attending a sports medicine conference (on improving your golf swing).

> *Dear Steve and Shona,*
>
> *Thank you for your participation in our contest. We regret to inform you that the entry "Nanotechnology in the Hospital Pharmacy" was the winner. While we certainly enjoyed seeing your entry, I doubt that we had as much fun as you guys did making it. We felt you deserved an honorable mention. Please accept this gift certificate as a token of our appreciation.*

The certificate was for a year's subscription for the *American Journal of Pharmacology*. Depressed, I took the letter to Shona. "We didn't win, Shona. I am sorry. Maybe we can try it again next year?" She looked at me with a sly little smile. "Stevie, I'm not sure you *lost* at all. The next time you enter that contest, you're doing it with Robert, the other pharmacist. There are a lot of people who want to see the both of you topless."

I haven't entered the competition since then, though I still have those photos on my laptop.

I really enjoy cooperation with other medical professionals – don't you?

—◊—

"After the general kicks in you won't even feel the bullet."

MARGARET.

'Come in, she said. I'll give you shelter from the storm.'
Bob Dylan.

Our society has an infatuation with youth. People are obsessed with acting young, feeling young, and looking younger. We actually don't want to age, and we certainly don't want to see other people growing older and getting sick. It reminds us of our own mortality. Most of us will likely be packed off to nursing homes, where we will stay out of sight.
Although we don't exactly want to be old or be thought of as old, the truth is that we will all grow old. The only alternative is dying young. Far from being some sort of burden on people, little old ladies do more for our society than we can ever imagine.
They are the living, breathing part of our societal history. They are also the last resort when their children run out of money or there are family problems at home. I can't tell you how many older women have come in and told me that their son, daughter, or grandkids have moved in with them. A divorce, a separation, or the loss of a job can force people to go back home. One's last and best safety net is often one's mom.
Perhaps more importantly, mothers are moral compasses. They tell us when we are doing something stupid or reckless. I like little old ladies. They are someone's wife, mother, and grandmother. Perhaps we run the risk of forgetting just how important these people are. The truth is that as a society, we must value what these people do. It's a heck of a lot

more important than money. Their work is a reflection of our civilization.

Margaret Stuart was a sensible woman. For each of the eight-two years of her life, she had always behaved properly. She liked to think of herself as a farm girl, but she had not lived on a farm for many years—not since she had gotten married at the age of twenty-one. This morning, she had to go to the doctor. Margaret put her boots and hat on quite carefully. She wanted to stay warm, and it was a cool November day outside. It was windy—almost blustery. She didn't want to go out today. It was too cold outside and she really didn't even want to go to the doctor. She was nervous—so nervous that she had developed tremblings and flutterings over the past week. They had bothered her so much that she had taken to having a glass of wine with her dinner. She was afraid that the doctor was going to give her bad news or that somehow he had detected that she had been consuming wine and needed to stop. She occasionally felt some heartburn. Was this anything to mention to the doctor? Her husband had recently died of bowel cancer. Every little complaint she had had since then seemed to be a prelude to cancer or some other frightful illness.

Margaret had two grown-up children who both had families of their own. They both worked and were often too busy to see her. Margaret had never owned a car. At eighty-two years of age, she didn't feel like learning to drive. She therefore bundled up and walked the five blocks to the doctor's office. Arriving at the office, Margaret was surprised to find that the little building was quite busy. It was flu season. At the doctor's office, they were installing a plastic shield over the secretary's desk. The secretary said that it was to protect her from people who coughed and spluttered at her. One flu victim even threw up in the office, narrowly missing the secretary. After that, all sorts of protective plastic shields were put in place, and they put up a sign that said, "Germs are the devil. Wash your hands!"

Margaret settled into one of the chairs in the waiting room. They were quite uncomfortable. Apparently, the hospital had had an operating room garage sale, and the doctor had picked them up for a song. Thankfully, she didn't have to wait for long. Margaret was ushered into room number one. Her chart was on the desk. She wanted to see what was on the chart. Was there secret information? A horrible thought occurred to her. Maybe the doctor knew that she had been drinking wine and he was going to refer her to Alcoholics Anonymous. The children would find out. The church choir would find out. As Margaret sat there, she became increasingly anxious. She could hear the doctor chatting with some other patient in the next room. She noted that her chart was the size of a Toronto telephone book. How had it gotten so thick? She desperately wanted to look at her chart. What had the doctor written about her?

In all of Margaret's life, she had always done as she had been told, and she really could not remember a time when she had broken the law or done anything even remotely sneaky. It just wasn't in her. She was the eldest of three daughters who had grown up on the farm, and her mother had been fond of whacking the kids with an old wooden spoon if they ever misbehaved. Her husband had also been a very orderly man. She had met him during the war. She was what they called a war bride. She had met her dashing husband when he had been stationed in England. He had somehow survived the bombing runs over Germany, and they had gotten married after the war. Canada seemed like the place to go, as England was a mess. She had never looked back. As she would say, she had become as Canadian as maple syrup.

With her husband gone and her kids away, she had lost many of the things that had anchored her life. She realized that she was fragile now and it scared her. What did her test results say? Was her liver going to shrivel up? Was her high blood pressure going to give her a stroke? Her friend Enid had high blood pressure, and her head was often so red and swollen that their friends thought it would pop off.

Knowing that you shouldn't be looking at your chart without permission from the doctor, she decided to do so anyway. It was the first time she had broken any sort of rule in many years. She opened the thick file and looked at a bewildering list of lab tests, something called an echocardiogram, a pulmonary function test, and a CAT scan of her head. She couldn't quite remember what all of these various tests were. Reading carefully, she came across a lab report in which the doctor had circled an abnormal result. Oh no! What was this? Her little heart was already beating very fast, but it began to beat even faster. Trying to read everything quickly, she pulled the thick chart closer and began to shuffle through the various chart notes. Just then, the doctor swooped into the room.

Oh my. The doctor had caught her red-handed. She was so stricken that she jumped up and tossed the chart contents all over the floor.

"Hi, Margaret. I guess you were curious. You were looking in your file."

"I am so terribly sorry, doctor. You see, it was right there and I was curious."

The doctor smiled, stooped over, and picked up the chart. She expected him to be angry. It was always a bad idea to cross a doctor. She had only started seeing this fellow when her husband had become sick. The doctor looked at her and then shuffled through the large chart. His expression became serious. He turned to her, looking at her carefully.

"You know, Margaret, I like your hat. Where did you get it?"

Margaret was flabbergasted. After all of her tests, including the abnormal one, he was asking about her hat? She didn't know what to say.

"Um, I think I may have purchased it at a millinery in Kingston. You know, doctor, I was looking through my chart and you had circled something."

"That's a nice warm-looking hat. Is it lined? I think it's quite stylish."

Margaret had become a little distracted about the hat. It was, after all, one of her favorites. It was made out of brown felt, and it had a leopard-print stripe on it. She always thought that it looked rather jaunty. Ruby, her friend from church, had helped her pick it out.

"Well, doctor, I picked it up at a store in Kingston."

"Do you mind telling me where? You see, I have to buy a hat for my mother. I think she would like a hat like that."

"Does your mother live in Kingston?"

"Actually, she lives in Toronto. She doesn't drive, so I am always worried about her keeping warm while waiting for the bus. I think that she should take taxis, but she thinks they cost too much money. The funny thing is that she has a good pension. I keep telling her that she has to look after herself. I think you get exposed to the flu a lot in the subway and on the bus."

They talked for a good half an hour about this and that. They talked about how children thought that money grew on trees and how the flu season had come on very strong this year. Finally, the doctor looked up and realized that he had been talking for too long.

"Um," he said. "There was something about your lab tests."

Margaret was just starting to relax when her stomach tightened into an uncomfortable knot. The doctor shuffled the papers in the files as he looked over them, checking each piece of paper carefully. Margaret braced herself for the bad news.

"I am afraid I have a little bad news for you."

"Oh?" By now Margaret's heart was thumping like a jackhammer.

"Yes. I found that your vitamin B12 levels are a little bit low.

"What does that mean, doctor? Am I sick? I don't want cancer!" She couldn't hide the quivering in her voice.

At this point, the doctor took her trembling hand into his. Her hands were cold from being outside, and she had trouble keeping them warm. He patted her hand to warm it, and he smiled at her.

"Margaret, you are doing just fine. You looked after your husband for all of those years; now it's time for you to look after yourself. All you have is a little vitamin deficiency. I am going to give you a vitamin supplement to take once a day. Maybe your mother gave you a vitamin pill when you were a kid."

"Well, doctor, my mother did give us Marmite sandwiches when we were kids."

"Marmite," he said. "Right. Actually, I think it has B vitamins in it. All you need is vitamin B12. Everything else is just fine. You take these vitamins and eat some fruit, vegetables, and some red meat. Don't skip any meals. I'll see you in a couple of months, but call me if you aren't feeling well."

On the way out, the doctor mentioned that he was going to get his mother a new hat just like hers. He told her to be careful, as it was a little slippery outside. Later that night, Margaret's daughter called her. She had been quite worried about her mother. Her mother had been really quite unsteady after her dad had died.

"Mom, how was the doctor's visit? Is everything OK?"

"Oh yes, dear. He really liked my hat. He wants to get one for his mother."

"He liked your hat? That was it?"

"He wants me to take some B vitamins and look after myself."

After Margaret left the office, the secretary came into the doctor's private office. "What took so long with Margaret? Is she sick of something?"

"No," said the doctor. "Actually, I think she's quite healthy. I thought she was going to worry herself into a tizzy, so I spent most of the time talking about her hat."

"Why didn't you just tell her that the tests were OK and then send her on her way."

"Oh, I don't know. I just thought she needed someone to talk to."

Later on that day I found myself listening to Bob Dylan and thinking about my own mother.

'Thank you mom'.

—⚏—

"Can you recommend a wine that goes well with
red meat, Zanex, and Lipitor?"

THE MEDICAL STUDENT

Linda, a first-year medical student, approached the undergraduate dean's office with some trepidation. The dean had a reputation for aloofness that was typical of doctors who did little actual medical care. His mild manner belied a holier-than-thou attitude that made most people feel inadequate. It was easy to feel inadequate when you were only a first-year medical student. Linda approached the office and realized that it wasn't all that nice. There was no secretary, and the office and hallway looked a bit old and tired. She knocked on the old oak door. Someone said, "Come in." She entered. The dean, a noted researcher who studied the elderly and the depressed, looked rather elderly and depressed himself. He was supposed to debrief her following her first in-hospital training session. He had not really approved of the idea of first-year students being allowed in a hospital; however, the university docs wholeheartedly welcomed the idea of sending the students away for as long as possible.

"Linda, it's nice of you to drop in. I thought we would have a little chat about your first hospital rotation...at Community Memorial, wasn't it?" Linda explained that this was not specifically a teaching hospital, but it did have a loose affiliation with another medical school. Her parents also lived near the hospital, which afforded her the opportunity to bike to work. "So, what was your experience like?"

"Well, sir, the elective was two weeks long. When I called the hospital, they fixed me up with two preceptors who worked in both the departments of anesthesia and family practice. I felt that this would provide some variety. The first doctor, Dr. G., was an intelligent and thoughtful teacher who provided a huge amount of insight into hospital based medicine. We had a variety of interesting cases, including several gallbladders and one case of congestive failure. I also got to practice starting IVs, and I learned how to anesthetize a patient. The whole experience was excellent. I think that I was able to learn about a variety of organ systems and anatomy."

The dean seemed pleased with what had happened, and he was about to conclude the interview. "You mentioned one of the preceptors. What about the other one?" "Oh, the other preceptor was OK." Not wanting to make a fuss, she had glossed over the other preceptor's performance, hoping the dean wouldn't notice. Unfortunately, he had. "Tell me about the other preceptor. Tell me about the second one, Dr. K."

The student took a deep breath to collect her thoughts about the week that she had endured with this particular doctor. "Well, the week began with my meeting Dr. K. in the operating room. Most of the time, rather than actually doing any learning activities, he sent me out to get doughnuts and lotto tickets from the women's auxiliary shop." Linda went on to relate that this didn't seem to be that useful of an occupation for a student. Curious, the dean asked, "How did the doctor respond to your remark? Did he focus more on learning activities?" "Actually, no he did not. His reasoning was that most Canadian doctors really never retire happily and that as a practicing doctor, winning the lotto was kind of his retirement plan. He encouraged me to purchase tickets also, but I really don't gamble."

Appalled, the dean asked if the preceptor had exhibited any other unusual behavior. Linda responded that aside from his continuous demands for doughnuts, coffee, and winning the lotto, he seemed to be preoccupied with things that were unrelated to medicine. The first thing that he obsessed about was getting on the *Oprah Winfrey Show*. He claimed that Dr. Phil was not a real doctor. He also kept touting an idea that he had come up with to deal with the numerous nurses who had been laid off in the province. "Oh, that's interesting," said the dean. "What was the doctor's plan?" "Actually, he wanted to start up a telephone and Internet sex line called *Naughty Nite Nurses*. He called this Canada's future high-tech industry." Linda went on to say that Dr. K. had emphasized repeatedly that no one had ever gotten an STD having phone sex; however, he was having difficulty getting anyone from the nursing staff to sign on for the job. He kept asking them to pose for pictures. I think they were becoming really annoyed with him."

The dean was a bit flabbergasted. "Look, is there anything this doctor did that had anything to do with medicine?" Linda, wanting to put the week behind her, said, "At one point, Dr. K. assessed a patient at the hospital to see if she would qualify for home oxygen. We were to do an arterial blood gas test." The dean, sounding relieved, said that this was the kind of thing he expected her to learn about. "The only thing, professor, was that prior to doing the blood test, he actually put a plastic bag over the patient's head and began chasing her around the room with an old mop. He said that it was the only way the Ministry of Health would qualify her for oxygen!" The dean, mortified, asked what had happened after that. Linda advised him that the terrified patient eventually collapsed. Dr. K. then took her blood sample—it was a rather deep blue color—and then resuscitated her with oxygen. This seemed to satisfy him a great deal.

Making notes about what had happened, the dean asked if there was anything else that he should know about the week, as he was going to make recommendations for future students regarding that particular hospital. "Dr. K. also had a frightening preoccupation with some sort of conspiracy theory involving the Ministry of Health and Community Memorial. He believed, quite honestly, that there was a plot to close his hospital and replace it with an office filled with Ministry of Health bureaucrats who would spend their time hiring computer consultants who would then hire more consultants. They would give it a fancy name like Canada Health Web."

Meanwhile, three hundred kilometers away, at Community Memorial...

"Steve, how was the week with the medical student? Did you teach her anything?" The hospital CEO had been pressuring us to take in medical students. The hospital management thought that this was a good way to try and recruit future doctors. "Oh, it was just great. I think she's going to be a great doctor. By the way, are you going to the coffee shop? I need a lotto ticket."

—m—

"It's a standard agreement stating that if for some reason you don't get better you wont tell anyone that I was your doctor."

GROWING OLD TOGETHER

I have often wondered what it is that successfully keeps marriages together. As a doctor, I have seen many marriages break up, but I have also seen many older people who have reached their fiftieth anniversaries. When you are a couple with many years of marriage under your belt, you start going to the doctor together. I appreciate this because I can get a better idea of what's going on with patients when there are two of them around. Perhaps one of the reasons that people come in together after a while is because they just can't manage without each other. They become like a peanut butter and jelly sandwich. You just can't have one without the other.

One day, Sally came in for her bimonthly visit with her husband, Frank. These folks lived on a farm that their son had taken over. Frank was semiretired but was still as busy as ever helping his kids. There was a problem that I could see right away. Frank's arm was in a sling. He looked a little unhappy and he was moving slow. In fact, Sally was moving kind of slowly also.

"What's up, guys? You both don't look so good. What happened?"

Frank said, "Well, doc, there was a problem and it has to do with what you told Sally during that last visit." I could not remember what I had told Sally during her last visit, so I consulted my chart. "Well, Frank, all I told Sally was that she should use something to moisturize her skin, as she was getting some peeling skin and an itchy rash."

"That's how this whole thing got started! My shoulder blade's broken now and my leg hurts also."

At this point, I was terribly confused and a little worried that I was going to get some sort of complaint lodged with the Ministry of Health. Frank warmed up to his story. I could tell that he wanted to recount what happened in great detail. This was probably so that he could assign fault and blame appropriately. Old married people are prone to doing this sort of thing.

"Well, doc, you told Sally she needed to moisturize. So, a couple of days later she went out and got some sort of cream for her skin. I told her that all she needed was some Vaseline, but she had to get the expensive stuff. Anyway, when that stuff didn't do the trick, she decided to take a bath with some baby oil to see if that would do the trick. Anyway, the oil reacted with the cream and she became so slippery that she couldn't get out of the bathtub. She kept sloshing around in there like a stranded baby whale or something."

At this point, Sally looked at him and said, "I did not slosh around like a baby whale! The tub is too big and it was very slippery!"

"Anyway, doc, Sal called for me and I came in to help her out of the tub. I got my hand around her wrist to help her up, when—darn it—my hand slipped off of her because she was so slippery. I then slipped on the wet floor and landed on my back, breaking my shoulder blade."

Sally then said, "It was just so awful, doc. We had to call an ambulance."

"It wouldn't have been so bad, but the cops showed up first and thought we were having some sort of wild sex party."

"Why was that?"

"They saw Frank's pecker pills," she said, referring to the erectile dysfunction tabs that I had previously given to Frank.

"Anyway, doc, the ambulance finally arrived and brought me to the hospital."

"OK, and what about you, Sally?"

"Oh, doc," said Frank. "They finally got her out of the tub using some sort of pneumatic device. I think they use something like it on the farm to lift up cows and such." When he said this, he snickered a bit. I tried not to laugh.

Sally didn't like it too much when Frank mentioned this. She had to have the last word. "Did Frank tell you how his leg got hurt? He has been so laid up with his shoulder that I've had to do everything for him lately. Anyway, he kept going on and on about the ambulance people helping me up. I really think he needed something else to talk about. The other day, there was this big horse-fly in the house. It landed on Frank's leg. I had to whack it. I guess I went at it too hard. His leg's hurting now too."

I looked at these two people who had been married for forty years. They were holding hands and smiling like a couple of kids.

I like a happy ending. Don't you?

Cheers,

—〰—

AFTERWORD

Dear readers.

Thank you for reading this book. I hope this book has helped you to laugh. Sometimes it's hard to find joy when you are facing difficult times. It is my wish that you find this book when you need it the most.

This book is dedicated to the volunteers and staff at Trenton Memorial Hospital. This institution is a little hospital in a small community that believes you don't have to be big to deliver excellent care.

A good doctor is someone who is a keen observer of the human condition. The practice of medicine has changed a great deal over the past 30 years; however, the idea that we should treat each other with respect and compassion will never go out of style. My colleagues are examples of empathy and professionalism. It is a real privilege to work with them.

Try and laugh everyday. It's easier than you think.

Sincerely,
Dr. Stephen M Kaladeen.

BOOK CLUB QUESTIONS:

1. This book is brilliant. How do I nominate the author for a Booker Prize?
2. The author's photo on the back cover shows a strikingly attractive middle-aged man. The phrase "silver fox" comes to mind. Has the picture been photo-shopped?
3. The author is Canadian. Are all Canadian men as sexy and photogenic?
4. Considering the author is so photogenic and witty, why isn't he on TV?
5. How can we recommend this book to Oprah?
6. Will the book club meeting supply free chocolate éclairs? If so, the author may appear in person just make sure there are enough for every one (two per person).

Stay tuned for the further work from Dr Steve.

CPSIA information can be obtained at www.ICGtesting.com
Printed in the USA
LVOW10s1223040516

486666LV00002B/253/P